Cheapskate's Guide to
Las Vegas

Other Books by Connie Emerson

Write on Target

How to Make Money Writing Fillers

Fodor's 1988 Fun in Las Vegas including Reno and Lake Tahoe

Writer's Guide to Conquering the Magazine Marketplace

The 30-Minute Writer

Cheapskate's Guide to
Las Vegas

Connie Emerson

A CITADEL PRESS BOOK
Published by Carol Publishing Group

Carol Publishing Group Edition, 1997

A Citadel Press Book
Published by Carol Publishing Group
Citadel Press is a registered trademark of Carol Communications, Inc.

Editorial, sales and distribution, rights and permissions inquiries
should be addressed to Carol Publishing Group, 120 Enterprise Avenue,
Secaucus, N.J. 07094

In Canada: Canadian Manda Group, One Atlantic Avenue, Suite 105,
Toronto, Ontario M6K 3E7

Carol Publishing Group books may be purchased in bulk at special
discounts for sales promotions, fund-raising, or educational purposes.
Special editions can be created to specifications. For details, contact
Special Sales Department, Carol Publishing Group, 120 Enterprise Avenue,
Secaucus, N.J. 07094

Manufactured in the United States of America
ISBN 0-8065-1844-8

10 9 8 7 6 5 4 3 2

Library of Congress Cataloging-in-Publication Data

Emerson, Connie, 1930–
    The cheapskate's guide to Las Vegas : hotels, gambling, food,
shows, and more / Connie Emerson. —Rev. and updated.
        p. cm.
    "A Citadel Press book."
    ISBN 0-8065-1844-8 (pb)
    1. Las Vegas (Nev.)—Guidebooks. I. Title.
F849.L3544 1996
917.93'1350433—dc20   96–25070
                                                  CIP

To Wilma McLeod
Who loves Las Vegas almost as much
as she loves finding a bargain

Acknowledgments

Every book has its unsung heroes, the people who provide missing pieces of information, suggestions, and moral support. Since I don't know the names of many fellow travelers whose tips became part of this book, they will, unfortunately, have to remain unacknowledged. But there are people I can thank: George Emerson, Ralph Emerson III, Ken Evans, Ann Henderson, Don Payne, John Reible; my editor, Allan J. Wilson, and the other people at Carol Publishing who worked on the project. I would also like to express my love and gratitude to my husband, Ralph, who never failed to give me encouragement when I needed it.

Contents

1. Introduction   1

Las Vegas is a great town when you have lots of money. But what do you do when you're darn near broke? Actually, you can have a pretty good time. In fact, Las Vegas may well be the bargain capital of the USA. The purpose of this book is to let you know what these bargains are and how to go about finding them.

2. Pre-trip Planning   6

You'll save a bundle in Las Vegas if you lay the groundwork before you leave home. Even how and what you pack can influence what you spend. To get off on the right traveling foot, read this chapter.

3. Accommodations   21

You can get a room for $100 or you can get one for $30. It might even be the same room. Whether you pay full rack rate or a fraction of it depends on a number of factors. If you know what they are, living in style on a budget isn't hard. We tell you how in seventeen easy pages.

4. Dining   33

Las Vegas is one of the world's bargain dining spots. No doubt about it. There are hundreds of places to eat in, however, and it isn't always a "you get what you pay for" situation. To take the bite out of your restaurant checks, read this chapter.

5. Attractions and Entertainment   51

Almost everyone who visits Las Vegas takes in a show or two. Some of these people stand in long lines and pay the full admission price.

Others get in for a discount. Still others walk right through the VIP line and don't pay a dime. This chapter turns the spotlight on maximizing your entertainment dollars.

6. Shopping/Souvenirs   80

Whether your taste runs to Lalique vases or Elvis on black satin, this chapter tells you where to go to find the best prices. It includes information on everything from bargain hunting at architectural-antiques auctions (care to bring home a spiral staircase?) to sale days at Saks.

7. Sightseeing   94

Some Las Vegas visitors never venture beyond the Strip. Others spend their entire stay in Glitter Gulch. But there are non-neon sights, too, such as Red Rock Canyon and Lake Mead; day trips to places like Laughlin and Pahrump. This chapter tells you about the most interesting spots and how to see them without spending a small fortune.

8. Getting Around   109

You like to ride in stretch limos, I know. But when you're pinching pennies, you search for cheaper transportation. And luckily, there's lots of it in Las Vegas. If you want to rent a car, you'll need to know where the best deals can be found. So we'll tell you that, too. And we'll even show you where to find bargains on the limos.

9. Strictly for Seniors   121

It may not be so great getting older. But for those long of tooth but short on cash, there are advantages in Las Vegas not available to anyone else. This chapter will tell you how to go about finding them.

10. Family Fun   132

You think Las Vegas is a Disney World for adults. You're right. But it can also be so much fun for youngsters that they'll forget about

Nintendo for the whole trip. Cutting costs at the theme hotels, on activities for the kids and on attractions the whole family will enjoy, will make paying the bills a lot more enjoyable, too.

11. When Is a Bargain Not One?   146

Okay, so they give you a free hat advertising their sportsbook. But only after you pony up $10 to bet on the horse races. Some of the so-called Vegas "bargains" are like that, so we'll show you what to look for...how to tell the money savers from the come-ons.

12. Sources and Resources   160

Since the freebie scene is ever changing, we'll tell you where to get current information on giveaways and good deals. And because your vacation time is often as precious as your money, this chapter also offers tips on bargain-hunting shortcuts,

13. Robbing the One-armed Bandits   173

We're not encouraging you to do anything illegal here. Just letting you in on the secrets of making the most of your gambling money. And while there are no guarantees, it's an odds-on bet that you'll have a much better chance of breaking even if you follow this chapter's advice.

14. Postscript   203

Introduction

Okay, so you *need* a vacation. Problem is, you and your traveling companions each can spend only $25 a day, after you've paid for getting to wherever you decide to go.

Better head for Las Vegas.

Or maybe you have unlimited funds to play with. But it galls you to pay $200 a night for your hotel room, and almost that much on dinner for two in a really fine restaurant.

Net worth has nothing to do with wanting to get the most for your money. So you had better consider Las Vegas, too.

I'll tell you all about it right now.

Las Vegas is glitzy, glamorous, gaudy. Flamboyant to a fault. Electronic pleasure palaces line its main artery. The sky shrieks with a kaleidoscope of colored tubing—reds, greens, blues, and golds whirling, flashing, pulsing; marquees splashed with the top names in the entertainment world. Signs advertise 99¢ breakfasts, free drawings, and round-the-clock check-cashing services. It's a twenty-four-hour town. Electric, exciting, addictive.

Inside the casinos, first-time tourists from Abu Dhabi to Dubuque gaze, mesmerized, at the strings of colored lights blinking nonstop around dollar slot-machine carousels, keno numbers flashing on the boards, roulette wheels spinning, crowds around the craps tables whooping it up, while Kenny Rogers's voice advises via Muzak that you gotta know when to fold 'em.

Cries of pleased surprise and "Yes!" keep reminding players whose piles of coin are dwindling that they, too, might hit it big if they just keep trying. Play a winning keno ticket. Hit a giant jackpot. Win the drawing for a luxury car or a dream vacation.

That's only one face of Las Vegas, the one layered with makeup and make-believe. Beyond the dazzle, it's a city with churches and parks and museums like other cities. But not quite. Because of the millions of tourists who visit each year, it boasts far more attractions and shops than most other metropolitan areas of similar size.

All of which enhances Las Vegas as a vacation destination both for people with lots of bucks and those who have to get along on $25 a day. But there's another factor as well that contributes to the city's allure for bargain hunters.

It's a paradox, I know, but while the gaming industry taketh away, it also giveth. Las Vegas hotel/casinos aren't like hotels in other parts of the country that have to rely on rooms, food, and beverage for their income. Because of the increased profitability of gambling casinos when their hotel rooms are filled to near capacity, hotels go to great lengths to keep occupancy rates up.

To entice people to stay at their properties, they offer rooms, meals, drinks, and entertainment at bargain prices. In some cases, they show a small profit or break even on meals and the like. At times, room rates, discounted meals, and cut-rate drinks are used as loss leaders.

Because of this phenomenon and the large number of casinos in Las Vegas competing for the tourists' dollars, the city is perhaps the ultimate vacation destination in the United States as far as getting the bang for your buck. Where else can you get a room in a four-star hotel for $49 or a steak and eggs breakfast for $1.99?

Back to the Beginning

The first settlement in Las Vegas (Spanish for "the meadows") occurred when the Mormon Church, headed by Brigham

Young, sent a mission of thirty men to construct a fort and teach agriculture to the Indians in the early 1850s. It wasn't to become a city, however, until 1905, after the Union Pacific Railroad announced that Las Vegas had been designated a major division point.

Even with the construction of nearby Hoover Dam in the early 1930s, Las Vegas remained a small town until after World War II. Although gambling had been legalized by the Nevada state legislature in 1931, it was confined to a few clubs in the downtown area and along the two-lane highway to Los Angeles. Then, on Christmas Day, 1946, Bugsy Siegel's Flamingo opened—most celebrated of the casinos on what would later become known as the Strip—and Las Vegas was on its way to becoming "The Entertainment Capital of the World."

Today, some forty-one major casinos line the Strip or are within easy walking distance, and an additional seventeen gambling palaces are located downtown in Glitter Gulch. With the opening of the MGM Grand Hotel, Casino & Theme Park in late 1993, Las Vegas could lay claim to having the ten biggest hotels in the world.

Las Vegas is the largest American city founded in the twentieth century. It's the only city that has its train depot at a casino. The only place where you can get married without getting out of the car.

Like Mecca for the Muslims—but for entirely different reasons—Las Vegas is a place most people feel that they should see at least once before they die.

Spread out over an area of 84.272 square miles (219.1 square kilometers), the city is located in a broad valley with lots of growing room left. The major automobile artery in and out of Las Vegas is Interstate 15 south to Los Angeles and north to Salt Lake City. U.S. 95 connects Las Vegas to Reno in the north and Phoenix to the south.

While Las Vegas is only the eightieth largest city in the United States, its airport, McCarran International, is as large as that of America's fourth-largest city, Houston. The tourist count for 1993 was somewhere between 22 and 23 million.

And the glitz and glitter keep on getting brighter. Theme resorts and theme parks are the order of the decade, with several big projects on the drawing boards. Because of legalization of gambling in an increasing number of states, Las Vegas is determined to keep its reputation as the gambling, as well as entertainment, capital.

Which brings us back to the purpose of this book—to help you find the deals that also make Las Vegas the bargain capital, if not of the world, at least of U.S. cities.

The book is divided into twelve chapters, each of which deals with a different area—accommodations, dining, sightseeing—in which bargains are available. Read the chapters in any sequence you like; skip those that may not apply to you. Use the book as a springboard to finding what seem like good deals to you.

For just as we have different views on politics and religion, we don't always see eye to eye as to what constitutes a bargain. You may think a hotel with a low rate and free tennis privileges is a value. I may be looking for that same low rate but with covered parking or an in-house business center.

The people who dream up the various hotel/casino promotions are aware that the millions who visit Las Vegas each year aren't cookie-cutter people. Each casino has an idea of what its potential clientele is generally like and of the kind of clientele it would like to attract.

This means that the freebies and discounts aren't necessarily going to be of value to everyone. As a result, although I have tried not to let my personal foibles get too much in the way, I may have omitted a bargain or two simply because they didn't seem like bargains to me.

Also, there's the matter of space. Books have a finite number of pages. And when you are writing about a place like Las Vegas, it's simply impossible to include everything. So one must choose.

While making my choices, I've kept in mind that although

it's great fun to get something for nothing, life doesn't often work that way. Some kind of action is usually demanded in return, even if it just means walking through a crowded casino when you would rather be walking outside. So I have done my best, when it's necessary, to evaluate whether the gain is worth any inconvenience.

The next best thing to getting something for nothing is to get a lot for a very little, and that happens somewhat more frequently. This is the area that's received my most concentrated attention, since my philosophy has always been that it's downright silly to pay $50 for anything you can get for $25. That $25 saved is $25 you can spend on something else.

As a result, parts of this book are about getting something for nothing. Other parts tell you how to get a lot for very little. All of the book is devoted to showing you how to get maximum value, whatever amount of time and money you have to spend.

Just keep remembering that though the best things in Las Vegas life may not be free, chances are you can get them at a discount.

Pre-trip Planning

Spontaneity is great. Going to a movie with five minutes' advance notice, taking off for the shopping mall on a whim, add fun and excitement to your life. But when your objective is bargain travel, in most cases you'll have a hard time saving money to the max when your planning is minimal.

So give yourself some time. Three months is okay. Four is even better. That way you'll be able to do the research that can translate into hundreds of dollars of savings, even on only a long weekend.

Savings Plan

The first step in maximizing your vacation money is to gather together all the information on Las Vegas that you can find (see chapter 12 for where to find it). You'll definitely want to get info on accommodations, because that's the area in which your biggest savings can be made.

Obtain as many brochures and rate sheets as you can, for while we all know that the rooms, gardens, and pool areas are photographed from their most flattering angles, pictures are still our best way of determining what the various hotels and motels look like.

You'll want to know about the city's casino and non-neon attractions, too, so you'll be able to prioritize their importance to you in terms of your desire to experience them and their respective costs. Too often when you haven't done your vacation homework, you'll learn that you missed the attraction you wanted most to see, simply because you were too late in finding out about it.

Valuable time and money can be saved by obtaining good maps—including one of the Las Vegas Citizens Area Transit (CAT) bus routes—in advance of your trip. With a bit of study, you'll be able to plan your days' activities to save time that might otherwise be spent backtracking because you were unfamiliar with the lay of the land.

Another important pre-vacation task is to review the terms of your auto insurance regarding rental vehicles if there's any chance you might rent a car anytime you're on your trip. Some credit cards automatically provide insurance if you use your card for the rental, so check to see if yours does.

For people who have disabilities or special needs that influence their travel, it's especially important to plan ahead. Las Vegas is more accessible than most cities, with the usual ramping, special public rest room facilities, and modified hotel rooms. One hotel, the Imperial Palace, has listening devices for hearing-impaired persons in its show room. Items available to guests upon check-in are telecommunications for the deaf (TDDs), closed-caption decoders for television sets, and Shake Awake alarm clocks. With 13 percent of its staff made up of people with disabilities, the hotel was named National Employer of the Year in 1991 by the President's Committee on Employment of People with Disabilities.

At Excalibur, a mobile hoist is available to assist disabled guests in getting in and out of the water in both the pools and the Jacuzzi. Ramps in the deck area provide unrestricted movement around the pools and easy access to the snack bar and towel station. A special guide to services for people with disabilities is available at McCarran Aiport and can be obtained from the Clark County Department of Aviation, McCarran Airport, P.O. Box 11005, Las Vegas, NV 89111; 702-739-7511.

Budgeting Your Money

At some time when you're planning your trip, you'll have to decide how much time and money you can afford to spend. Though the average Las Vegas visitor spends three to four nights and around $275 per four-day trip, exclusive of accommodations, shopping, and gambling, you can have a great time for a lot less because the average visitor probably doesn't know how (or care) to get the most for his or her money.

Budgets are such individual affairs that we don't want to go into any specifics about what you can expect to spend except to caution you to be realistic. It might well cost a good amount if you fail to bring along sufficient cash or traveler's checks to cover what you'll need.

While there are about 200 Cirrus ATMs (800-4-CIRRUS) and almost 250 PLUS ATMs (800-THE-PLUS) in Las Vegas, hotel/casinos almost never cash the personal checks of anyone who isn't a hotel guest.

The Las Vegas banks that are affiliates of bank holding companies with offices in various parts of the country will cash out-of-state checks, but only for people who have accounts at member banks or with other affiliated banks. These are First Interstate Bank and Bank of America, both of which have several branches located in various parts of the city.

Two pieces of identification, including a driver's license and bank check-cashing card or major credit card, are necessary at First Interstate Bank, where the credit limit is $300 a day. At Bank of America, limits vary from $100 a day up to $1,000, depending upon the type of identification you have and the banking agreements between your home bank and B of A in Nevada.

To get cash advances from charge cards is expensive. Posted rates on machines range from $5.95 to $9.95 for any amount up to $100; with $95.95 to $99.95 the tariff for obtaining $1,000.

There are check-cashing services, too, if all else fails and you're desperate, but they charge a gigantic 20 percent on amounts up to $500, and you must have a major credit card plus a driver's license in order to cash the check.

Flight Time

Chances are, one of your biggest expenditures will be for airfare, since nearly half of Las Vegas travelers arrive via commercial and charter airlines.

Among the airlines currently flying regular schedules to and from Las Vegas are:

Alaska Airlines	800-426-0333
American and American Eagle	800-433-7300
America West	800-235-9292
Canadian Airlines International	800-426-7000
Continental	800-525-0280
Delta and Delta Connection	800-221-1212
Frontier Airlines	800-432-1359
Hawaiian Airlines	800-367-5320
Markair	800-627-5247
Midwest Express	800-452-2022
Northwest and NW AirLink	800-225-2525
Reno Air	800-736-6247
Southwest Airlines	800-435-9792
TWA	800-221-2000
United/Lufthansa	800-241-6522
USAir/British Airways	800-428-4322

You've heard time and again about paying $748 for a ticket, then sitting next to a guy who paid $289 for his. And yeah, he's the one who's not in the middle seat.

The reason you've heard this sad song so often is that it happens. A lot. By planning early, you can shop around for the best deals (or have a good travel agent do it for you). You'll also get your choice of aisle or window seat when you check in for your flight ahead of the mob—or better yet, arrange your seating in advance.

Like anyplace else, you're most apt to come upon the best airfares to Las Vegas when a new airline comes to town, or when a route war is going on and airlines drop fares to stay with the competition.

One of the best ways to anticipate these fare drops is to keep in touch with friends who work in the airline industry. They often hear rumblings before the fares are actually lowered. On occasion, the *Wall Street Journal* also carries news of fare breaks before they happen.

Check airline ads in the Sunday travel and entertainment sections of newspapers published in gateway cities closest to where you live. Sometimes, promotions are advertised in weekday editions, too. Fast action is required to take advantage of these deals as the tickets are available for only a short time or their number is limited.

In addition to the regularly scheduled commercial flights, two airlines operate more than 65 percent of the Las Vegas charter flights. They are Sun Country (800-359-5786), with regular flights out of Kansas City, Minneapolis, St. Louis, San Antonio, and Tulsa; and American Trans Air, Inc., which operates flights from Indianapolis and Chicago.

Among the less well-known sources for discounted airline tickets are bucket shops and bartered travel.

Bucket Shops. Airlines don't want to lose money, and every unsold seat on a flight is one that they aren't getting anything for. Therefore, when they anticipate light loads on various routes, the airlines sell blocks of tickets at greatly reduced rates to wholesalers, who in turn sell their unsold inventory to discounters. Airlines also sell these tickets directly to travel agencies that specialize in discounting.

These so-called bucket shops used to have a fly-by-night (pardon the pun) reputation, but as years have passed, most bucket shops have become reliable business operations. You'll find their advertisements in the travel sections of Sunday newspapers.

Discounted tickets often come without some of the requirements for tickets bought from the airlines, such as advance purchase. But this is often counterbalanced by other restrictions. Discounted tickets are almost always nonendorsable, which means that they can be used only on the issuing airline, so when a flight is canceled, you're out of luck until there's space on one of that airline's subsequent flights. Also, most of the tickets are stamped "nonrefundable," so they cannot be returned for a refund of the list price.

Before you advance any money, it's a good idea to check with the Better Business Bureau if you have any doubts regarding a discounter. And if it's possible, pay with a credit card rather than by check or money order.

Two consolidators offering discounted fares are Maharaja/Consumer Wholesale Travel, 34 W. 33rd Street, Suite 1014, New York, NY 10001; 212-213-2020 in New York, 800-223-6862 elsewhere in the United States; and TFI Tours International, 34 W. 37th Street, 12th floor, New York, NY 10018; 212-736-1140 in New York, 800-745-8000 elsewhere in the United States.

Another course of action—and this is one that defies the rule that booking flights early saves you money—is to utilize discount travel clubs. Simply put (and it's a fairly complicated subject), travel suppliers (the wholesalers who buy blocks of tickets from airlines, hotels, and the like) are often left with unsold inventory. Naturally, they would like to get some money back on this part of their investment, even if it's much less than they would usually receive. Discount travel clubs help the suppliers get rid of the inventory by offering complete tour and cruise packages, seats on charter flights, and occasionally, seats on scheduled flights at a fraction of their regular prices—from 15 to 60 percent off, in most cases—to their members on a "last-minute" basis (actually it can be a week or even a month in advance). In exchange for yearly membership fees, which are generally from $20 to $50, members are given access to a toll-free hotline number to call regarding last-minute travel bargains. Some clubs also send newsletters to their subscribers, telling about current offers.

Among the discount clubs now offering Las Vegas airline tickets are:

Encore/Short Notice, 4501 Forbes Boulevard,
Lanham, MD 20706; 301-459-8020.

Last Minute Travel, 1249 Boylston Street,
Boston, MA 02215; 800-LAST-MIN.

Traveler's Advantage, P.O. Box 1015,
Trumbull, CT 06611; 800-255-1488

Traveler's Advantage, 3033 S. Parker Road, Suite 1000
Aurora, CO 80014; 800-548-1116.

Bartered Travel. This is another source of discounted airline tickets. Airlines barter seats on their planes for hotel rooms and meals. Food wholesalers accept cruises in lieu of cash. Newspapers trade advertising space for airplane tickets and rental cars. But sometimes the hotels, food brokers, and newspapers find themselves with a surplus of the items they've traded for. So they sell these items to barter clubs at deeply discounted rates. Barter-club members pay an annual fee of about $50, which allows them to take advantage of these surplus accommodations and flights. Most of these operations seem to have a short life span, but one that has been around for several years is Travel World Leisure Club, 225 W. 34th Street, Suite 2203, New York, NY 10122 (800-444-TWLC).

However you choose to fly, pay for your ticket with your charge card if by so doing your bags are automatically insured.

Other Ways of Getting There

Las Vegas visitors who like train travel can hop aboard Amtrak, since one Desert Wind arrives from Salt Lake City and another from Los Angeles each day. Whether you consider the rail trip a bargain will depend upon the distance you have to travel, overnight accommodations you'll have to arrange for, meals you'll have to buy at rather hefty prices, and the psychic gratification you'll receive from riding the rails.

You can get to Las Vegas by bus, too. The city is served by Greyhound, and the terminal next to Jackie Gaugan's Plaza on Main Street is centrally located in the downtown area. The cheaper bus fares have to be balanced against the same factors as with railroad travel. Travel by charter bus is another matter and is covered later in this chapter under "Packaged Travel."

About 47 percent of Las Vegas visitors come by automobile or recreational vehicle. Whether this is a money saver or not depends upon how far away you live and whether you have the time to spend in traveling. Unlike hotels in most cities, most of the resorts and casinos in Las Vegas don't charge for overnight parking, and RV campgrounds are relatively inexpensive (see chapter 3).

Getting Your Zzzzzzzzzzs

Even people who plan to party all night need to book a room in Las Vegas. After all, you gotta sleep sometime. But that doesn't mean you have to sleep at the hotel's top rates.

For the past few years, the Las Vegas Convention & Visitors Authority has attempted to mold the city into a destination with no seasonal highs and lows. They have aimed, by attracting conventions and promoting special events, to keep the tourist count as consistent as possible throughout the year. And to a great extent, they've succeeded.

As a result, there's no real off-season, except from mid-November through January with the exception of National Finals Rodeo week and the days before and including New Year's.

At times of the year it's virtually impossible to be assured of getting a room unless you book several months in advance. But—good news to bargain travelers—there are days of the week and times of the year when hotels and motels charge a good deal less for their rooms in order to maintain occupancy levels.

You can save money if you are flexible as to the days/dates you'll stay in Las Vegas. By studying the information you've gathered on accommodations, you can determine when you'll get the most favorable rates at places that seem to meet your requirements best.

Combining your hotel/motel information with the locations of the various properties on your maps is important, too. Other things being equal, you'll want to choose the lodging place that's closest to the attractions you want most to visit. That way you'll save both time and money on transportation.

Packaged Travel

Many visitors to Las Vegas come via package tours. And it's no wonder. Some of the tours are available at incredibly low prices. The reason is that casinos and airlines charge tour operators very low rates, which they, in turn, pass on in part to their customers. In some cases, casinos go so far as to subsidize the operations, paying tour operators for each tour participant, providing rooms, meals, and other amenities.

The following are some of the companies that operate Las Vegas tours:

American Express Travel Related Services, 800-241-1700. Wholesaler.

Canadian Holidays, 1200 W. 73rd Avenue, Suite 500, Vancouver, BC V6P6G5, 800-661-8881

Dixieland Tours & Cruises, 8352 W. El Cajon, Baton Rouge, LA 70815, 800-256-8747. Tours leave from Louisiana locations.

Domenico Tours, 751 Broadway, P.O. Box 144, Bayonne, NJ 07002, 800-554-8687. Motorcoach tours.

Las Vegas Connection, 11010 Spring Hill Drive, Spring Hill, FL 34608, 800-628-3427. Tours leave from Florida. Retails to general public.

Mayflower Tours, 1225 Warren Avenue, P.O. Box 490, Downers Grove, IL 60515, 708-960-3430 inside Illinois, 800-323-7604 elsewhere in the United States. Sells directly to the public.

MLT Vacations, 5130 Highway 101, Minnetonka, MN 55345, 800-328-0025. Wholesales to travel agents. Tours leave from Dallas, Denver, Des Moines, Minneapolis, Omaha, St. Louis, San Antonio, and Tulsa.

MTI Vacations, 1220 Kensington Court, Oak Brook, IL 60521, 800-3232-7285. Wholesales to travel agents. Tours leave from Chicago, Milwaukee, and St. Louis.

Sunquest Vacations, 130 Merlon Street, Toronto, Ontario M4S1A4, 416-485-1700.

Globetrotters/SuperCities, 139 Main Street, Cambridge, MA 02142, 800-333-1234. Wholesaler. Tours originate in various cities.

A number of package tours are offered by the airlines serving Las Vegas. They include:

American Airlines FlyAway Vacations, Southern Reservations Center, Mail Drop 1000, Box 619619, Dallas/Ft. Worth Airport, TX 75261-9619, 800-321-2121.

America West Vacations, 1150 E. University, Suite 201, Tempe, AZ 85281, 800-356-6611.

Continental's Grand Vacations, P.O. Box 1460, Milwaukee, WI 53201-1460, 800-634-5555.

Delta's Dream Vacations, P.O. Box 1525, Ft. Lauderdale, FL 33302, 800-872-7786.

Northwest World Vacations, 5101 Northwest Drive, St. Paul, MN 5511-3034, 800-692-8687.

TWA Getaway Vacations, 10 E. Stow Road, Marlton, NJ 08053, 800-GETAWAY.

As you'll see from the list, some charter tour companies deal only with travel agents, who in turn either guide their clients in choosing a charter or put together charter tours for specific groups.

These groups run the gamut from depositors at the local savings and loan to the Sons of Norway. You often don't have to be a member of the sponsoring group to go on the charter. You may just be a friend of a member, or in some cases, all you need to be is a warm body to fill an unsold seat on the plane.

Some of these packages cost less than $400, including airfare and three or four nights' hotel accommodations. For example, when Ball State University played in the 1993 Las Vegas Bowl, charter tour-package prices from Indiana were as low as $375.

Charter tour companies that deal directly with the general public put together flights and then advertise them in newspapers and/or send out mailers to previous passengers.

What's included for the price you pay varies widely. Some charters involve little more than air transportation; others cover air transport, airport transfers, accommodations, all meals, and sight-seeing.

Profitable Packing

I once read an article about a woman who went around the world with only a large handbag for luggage. I don't recall exactly what she had in that bag, but I do remember that her nightgown doubled as a cocktail dress.

Now, I'm not suggesting that you drink your glass of white wine wearing the same outfit you slept in the night before, but I am saying that traveling light may save you enough money to buy that white wine—and lots of other things as well. So determine how much weight you can comfortably carry for a mile and then pack accordingly.

But how can packing light save me money? you ask. Well, for starters, say you've come to Las Vegas because two days ago you were able to buy airline tickets at half price. But you've no idea where you'll stay.

Since you and your companion are each carrying only one light bag, you can walk to the airport bus stop and hop on the bus to the Strip or Glitter Gulch for $1 instead of taking a shuttle or taxi. That's saved you a total of from $4.50 to $10 already, without counting the tip.

When you get off the bus at the first hotel that looks good, walk in and check it out. If it's not what you want, go on to the second one on your list, or even the third. When you're tired and loaded down with luggage, you'll be inclined to take the first room you can find, even if the price is beyond what you've budgeted.

What's in It?

You may not have thought much about the importance in the money-saving scheme of things of what you pack in your bag unless at some time in your travels you've had to buy toothpaste from a hotel vending machine or a pair of overpriced sunglasses from the gift shop in the shopping arcade. What you'll need on your trip will have a lot to do with the weather, so it's a good idea to know what to expect. Though the weather in Las Vegas can produce surprises, it's generally consistent from year to year. Here's a chart with the average daily maximum and minimum temperatures in degrees Fahrenheit by month.

January	54	34
February	59	35
March	66	42
April	81	54
May	90	63
June	102	72
July	105	78
August	104	75
September	87	62
October	80	54

| November | 62 | 40 |
| December | 60 | 36 |

Although the sun shines an average of 312 days a year, the weather isn't always perfect. While some days between Thanksgiving and the end of January are the shirtsleeve variety, others can be so cold that you're miserable without a warm jacket. It's not so pleasant either on the occasional March afternoon when dust, sex-for-sale handbills, and candy-bar wrappers swirl down Las Vegas Boulevard, or on the hottest summer days when the mercury hovers around 115° F.

Keep in mind, also, that Las Vegas is located in the desert and usually has very low humidity. So even if temperatures soar, you won't feel the heat as much as you would in the East, South, or Midwest. However, because of the heat, some buildings have air-conditioning systems that make you feel like you're in a meat locker. As a result, you'll be happier if you pack a sweater or jacket, no matter what time of year it is.

As far as the rest of your wardrobe is concerned, in Las Vegas just about anything goes. People wear everything from tuxedos and beaded gowns to jogging suits and T-shirts to the big production shows. You'll probably feel most comfortable, however, if you dress somewhere in between the two extremes.

Remember that you're in town to see the sights, not to be one of them. If you wear the same outfit five days in a row, it's likely no one will notice or care.

You will, however, want to pay special attention to choosing the shoes you'll bring along. My eighty-four-year-old aunt insists on wearing high heels. And since her passion is playing the slot machines, she gets along just fine. On the other hand (or foot, if you will), I want to see all the sights, so I wear the scruffiest, most comfortable shoes in my closet. I always have a supply of moleskin strips in my pocket, too, so that whenever I feel a spot becoming tender, I can put the moleskin over it *before* a blister develops.

There are a number of items you might pack that will be

worth many times their weight in savings. Plastic margarine tubs, plastic glasses, plastic cutlery, and a can opener (the type you buy for picnics that can open bottles as well) will let you breakfast and lunch on cereal, berries, cottage cheese, and other items from the grocery store.

The articles in an emergency kit (a few Band-Aids, pain reliever, needle and thread, digestive tablets, sunblock) may not necessarily be used, but if they are, will save you dollars. Put the items in a plastic storage bag with gripper closing so that you can find them easily if the need arises.

And don't forget your sunglasses and a hat. An extra copy of your eyeglasses prescription, tucked in your wallet, may come in handy, too. Fortunately, you won't need mosquito repellent unless you plan your trip for the first couple of weeks in June. It's too hot during the rest of mosquito season for the insects to live.

If you plan to make any bring-home purchases in Las Vegas, consider wearing and packing clothes that you would otherwise give to Goodwill. Leave the clothes behind in your hotel wastebasket and you'll have extra room in your suitcase. Otherwise, pack a lightweight carry-on bag in your luggage.

Las Vegas Lingo

So you'll sound like a native when you arrive, here are some terms you may want to incorporate into your vocabulary:

boxman—the craps-table dealer who sits over the drop box and supervises bets and payoffs

comp—short for free or complimentary

drop box—a locked box on the gambling table into which the dealer deposits paper money

high roller—a customer with the reputation of wagering large amounts of money in the casino

in red—comped customer's name usually appears in red pencil on the maître d's reservations chart

limit—the minimum or maximum bet accepted at a gambling table

marker—an IOU to the casino by a gambler allowed to play on credit

pit boss—a casino employee who oversees the table dealers in a gambling area

RFB comp—complimentary room, food, and beverage

shoe—the container from which several decks of cards are dealt

shooter—the gambler who is rolling the dice on a craps table

stickman—the dealer who moves the dice around on a craps table with a hook-shaped stick

toke—a tip or gratuity

3

Accommodations

The story is told of a man and a woman who spent fifty nights in Las Vegas hotels and had to pay for only one. All the rest were comps (complimentary) from hotel/casinos where they had gambled in the past.

It's a great story, but not the sort of thing that happens to most of us. Getting a room for 30 to 50 percent off the rate regularly charged for it, however, is a possibility for anyone who takes the time to become familiar with the Las Vegas hotel/motel room scene.

In 1996, New York-New York, Monte Carlo, Orleans, and Stratosphere plus expansions at three major properties added an amazing number of guest rooms—12,615—to the city's supply, bringing the total to somewhere around 100,000. And the construction momentum shows few signs of slowing down. Although the number of guest rooms keeps increasing, so does the tourist count, which reached somewhere around 30 million in 1996. And that's the conservative estimate.

Traditionally, Las Vegas hotel and motel rooms have higher occupancy rates than those in most other major tourist destinations—hotel/motel rooms have an average year-round occupancy of 89 percent, with 93 percent on weekends. Despite hotel/resort building booms, this high-occupancy trend is like to continue. And because of a reason that is good news for bargain-minded tourists.

You see, Las Vegas hotel/casino management abhors a

vacuum, i.e., empty hotel rooms. That's because every hotel room occupant over the age of twenty-one means a potential customer in the casino downstairs—where the property's *real* revenue is generated.

Therefore, rates fluctuate with demand—anything to keep those rooms full. As a result, at times the discounts are far deeper than is customary within the hotel industry as a whole.

Not only are there lots of rooms in Las Vegas. Talk about choices. Depending upon your taste and the size of your bankroll, you can relax in a penthouse suite complete with five bedrooms, crystal chandeliers, and butler, or stay in a room that contains little more than a bed, two chairs, and a TV. You can reserve a snazzy mini-suite with Jacuzzi in one of the leading hotels on the Strip or book a cozy motel room just down the street.

Actually, the penthouse may not be rentable. Most hotel casinos reserve them for high rollers—the people who gamble with a stake of half a million or so during a weekend. All of the other rooms and suites, however, can be had for a price—and that price can vary so widely that the modest rooms during prime convention time can cost about as much as the mini-suites go for during periods management considers to be relatively slow.

What accommodations you get for your money depends a lot upon the effort you spend in scoping out the various alternatives. It's not an assignment for the faint of heart, for the rate structures can be exceedingly complicated. For example, though some lodging places (primarily big hotel/casinos) have the same published rates year-round, most hotel and motel rates vary with the time of year.

To confuse matters further, it seems that properties with variable rates have differing ideas as to what constitutes their high and low seasons. Whereas some places charge less from June through September, others raise their rates at that time of year. By and large, however, you'll find the consistently lowest rates from mid-November through Christmas and the very highest on New Year's Eve and the days preceding or following (depending on the day of the week January 1 occurs). But again, some properties offer their rooms over New Year's Eve at the lowest rates.

In addition to New Year's, the times you'll have the least room for economic maneuvering are those dates when major conventions are in town. Two of the biggest are Consumer Electronics in January and Comdex in November.

Even deciding which days of the week you'll be in town can make a great deal of difference as to what you'll pay for your hotel or motel room. Those properties with seasonal rates—and a number that don't have them—almost always charge more for rooms on Friday and Saturday nights than they do Sunday through Thursday. And we're not talking just a little more expensive. You can generally save from 20 to 30 percent on lodgings by planning a midweek visit, no matter what time of year.

Working these two factors in combination, you'll find that if you're able to visit Las Vegas midweek during a season that your chosen hotel considers a slow time, you'll be able to save up to 50 percent. At one typical noncasino property, for instance, rooms that cost $40 five days before New Year's go for $78 four days after.

Or take Harrah's, rated a three-diamond property by AAA, with a terrific location on the central part of the Strip. Rates for two people/two beds start at $149 on Friday and Saturday nights from February 12 through May 30 and from September 3 through November 4. They start at $50 less on other weekends. A rather sizeable savings. But wait.

On Sunday through Thursday during Harrah's high seasons, the same rooms often go for $55, while on Sunday through Thursday the rest of the year, they're just $50. This means that unless you're conscious of how the hotel's rate structure works, you would most likely pay three times the price for the same room if you booked it for one of the high-range weekends than if you stayed in it on a couple of the low-range weekdays.

At the three-diamond Holiday Crowne Plaza, you can save even more. Two-person/two-bed suite rates drop from $215 during the most expensive period, January through April, to $112 during the lowest, October 15 to December, except for times when big conventions or busy weekends increase demand. Although the hotel's off-Strip location is a drawback to some tourists, it's a bonus for others.

Making Arrangements

Travelers who aren't comfortable unless they have room reservations months in advance usually get the lowest rates in Las Vegas, especially if their travel dates are flexible. That's because—despite the general seasonal/weekend swings in room prices—rates can fluctuate hourly. And according to a room-reservations person who has worked in Las Vegas for thirty-four years, it has always been that way. "I've seen rates go from the lowest to the highest in an hour because a big convention has been booked in and there aren't many rooms available," she says. However, rates for people who already have reservations for the dates affected, she adds, remain at the lower rate.

Chapter 12, "Sources and Resources," contains a list of the major hotel/casinos and their toll-free numbers. Use them not only to make your reservations, but to do some price comparisons beforehand.

According to the experts, if you phone a hotel/casino and request a room for one weekend night only, chances are you'll be told there are no vacancies. Since weekends are prime time as far as profitability is concerned, hotel management is loathe to break up potential two-day reservations. Even when you want a room from Wednesday through Friday nights, don't be surprised if only Wednesday and Thursday are available.

You'll find that rooms at hotel/casinos almost always are less expensive than the same-quality rooms in motels. The reason is simple. Motels have to make money on their rooms. Hotels don't. They can absorb costs for debt repayment, maintenance, and daily operation into their overall expense structure, since every occupied room means potential casino customers.

When you phone, ask if the price quoted is the best possible rate and if there are any discounts on it. Ask, too, what the price includes and if the hotel is currently offering any package deals. You may find that you pay the same for the room as the price that was given you when you began the conversation, but that you'll get a lot of extras as well.

What these extras are varies from hotel to hotel, so it's important to find out about as many different packages as you can. That way you'll be able to choose the deal that contains the extras that are most appealing to you.

For example, the Flamingo Hilton offers their Bounce Back package for $39 per person. It includes one night's room (double occupancy); the "Radio City Rockettes" production show with two drinks per person or dinner in the hotel's Garden Buffet Restaurant; one breakfast; two cocktails at the bar; and a funbook containing casino gambling coupons as well as discount coupons on food and merchandise.

Good Monday through Thursday, the package costs $6 more per person between the first of March and mid-May and from the first of September to mid-November, based on availability. Regular per night rates at the Flamingo Hilton for the least expensive double rooms go from $69 to $169 depending on occupancy projections at the time of booking.

Another Flamingo Hilton package, the "Flamingo Fling," costs $96 per person double occupancy from January 2 through December 26, 1996. It includes two nights' tower room accommodations, all the features of the "Bounce Back" package plus a free visit to the health spa and payment of the bellman gratuity on arrival.

Comparing the two packages, you'll see that the "Bounce Back" is the better deal for everyone but those who want to use the hotel's sauna, steam room and exercise facilities.

The Flamingo's sister hotel, the Las Vegas Hilton, offers a $98 per couple "Show and Room" package that includes one

Bargains—Without Reservations

While booking well in advance is usually your best bargain bet, waiting until the last minute doesn't always mean you'll have to pay top prices. Although rooms are virtually unavailable in Las Vegas at times, that isn't the case during much of November, December, and January. The important information you need before deciding on a spur-of-the-moment trip can be obtained by calling the Las Vegas Convention and Visitors Authority (702-892-0711) to find out whether the town is sold out.

If your timing is right, you'll improve your chances of saving money by doing something like this: Upon arrival at McCarran International Airport, go to the information desk on the ticketing level and get the names of hotels with available rooms. Unless you learn that rooms are in short supply, don't make the reservation by phone. Instead, write down the names of those hotels in your price range that sound most appealing.

Go in person to the first one on your list. Approach the front desk and ask if there are any discounts available—automobile club, senior, corporate—on their rooms that cost $35 or $40 or whatever price you've been quoted at the airport. A business card is a help in qualifying for the corporate rate even though you don't work for one of the companies the hotel deals with on a regular basis.

If you're traveling light and can't get a discount at the first hotel on your list, just go on to the next one. Chances are, especially in late afternoon when there are a lot of unsold rooms in town, most of them will be happy to lower their rates if you provide them with any halfway legitimate reason to do so. Remember that when room prices fluctuate with demand, they can move down as surely as they move up.

People who arrive by automobile, if they're wise, will have called a bunch of 800 numbers in advance and written down rates at the various hotels so they have three or four places targeted as possibilities. Nothing's worse when you've driven for eight hours with kids fighting in the backseat than to arrive at your destination during rush hour with no idea of where you'll stay that night. If you've come unprepared, try to find accommodations off the Strip and look for something closer on the next day.

---

night's lodging and two tickets to Starlight Express. Since the tickets are in the $32 category and hotel room rates start at $89, the package is clearly a money-saver for people who are anxious to see the show. The package is based on availability and is rarely available—needless to say—when rooms are going for more than the $89 rate.

MGM's "Grand Adventures" package includes one night's deluxe accommodations, the Oz buffet breakfast ($6.75 regular price) for two and two Grand Adventures wristbands that entitle their wearers to unlimited rides and attractions at the theme park. The package price ranges from $118 to $150, depending on season and availability.

The EFX package ($198 to $238) covers one night's deluxe accommodations, two Oz buffet breakfasts and two tickets to the MGM Grand's super spectacular EFX. If purchased separately, the price of one ticket is $70.

Perhaps you've noted that every package mentioned is based on availability. This is a good reason to book packages early if you want to be sure to get a deal. When you don't mind gambling on availability, you can often save even more by taking advantage of last-minute specials advertised in the travel or entertainment sections of metropolitan newspapers.

"Free" Nights Through Slot Clubs

Getting back to the forty-nine free nights story, it didn't tell how much money the couple spent gambling on previous trips to get all those complimentary room nights. But I have an idea that, unless they were very skilled gamblers and exceedingly lucky to boot, it cost a lot.

We'll talk about slot clubs in greater detail in chapter 13 "Robbing the One-armed Bandits," but as far as free rooms are concerned, you usually get them in one of two ways, depending upon the rules of the particular casino's program.

1. Your points accumulate on a slot-club card, which you insert into a box attached to the machine you are playing. When you have accumulated the required number of points, you can redeem them for various premiums, one of which at some of the casinos is free hotel nights.

For example, a two-thirds-page advertisement in one recent airline in-flight magazine began: "Gamble 4 hours on the Island and get 2 free nights in paradise." The ad promised people that if they signed up as new members of Tropicana's Winners Club and played slots or table games for four hours, they would receive two free weekday or weekend nights.

2. Casino slot-club personnel keep track of their members' hours of play/points accumulated per visit. At some casinos, all slot-club members are sent mailouts advertising various promotions, such as rooms at highly reduced rates (or, on occasion, free rooms). These rooms are subject to availability, generally during times when the hotel anticipates lower than normal occupancy.

Customer Service

The time comes in every traveler's life when his or her prepaid hotel or motel room is less than satisfactory. Should this happen to you with your Las Vegas room—bargain or not—you won't get the most for your money unless you speak up.

Maybe the cleaning person has done a poor job. Or the air-conditioning doesn't work properly. If your complaint is legitimate, the problem will almost always be taken care of quickly if you go to the front desk and ask to see the manager—or an assistant manager if the manager isn't on duty. Don't settle for less than the person in charge of the hotel at that time.

When for some reason you don't seem to be getting results, keep your voice calm but raise the volume so hotel guests in the vicinity can't help but hear you. This technique almost always works because managers know guest dissatisfaction can spread when unhappy guests start broadcasting their displeasure. If you can, when reserving a room, use your credit card to guarantee only the first night. That way, if the accommodations prove to be totally hopeless, you can move the next day without penalty.

RV Roundup

Travelers who carry their shells on their backs flock to Las Vegas. Not only are there a number of large recreational-vehicle parks in the area, there's also an escape hatch if all the parks are full. By driving an hour and a half south to Laughlin, RVers can park their rigs for free in the casinos' parking lots.

Most of the time, however, when arriving early in the day, RV travelers won't have a problem finding space in Las Vegas. The following are only a sampling of the almost three dozen parks in the city and immediate surroundings:

Boulder Lakes RV Resort & Country Club
6201 Boulder Highway
Las Vegas, NV 89122

702-435-1157
Daily—$18.90, including tax
Weekly—$113.40, including tax
Ten percent discount to AAA members paying cash on daily
rate
417 hookups, laundry and shower facilities, pool, convenience store

Oasis
2711 W. Windmill Lane
Las Vegas, NV 89123
702-260-2020
Daily—$12 to $21
Discount on monthly stays
One month maximum stay
702 full hookups, laundry and shower facilities, two pools,
Jacuzzi, convenience store, golf course, exercise facility

Circusland RV Park
500 Circus Circus Drive
Las Vegas, NV 89109
702-794-3757
Sunday–Thursday—$12.72 per day, including tax
Friday, Saturday—$16.96 per day, including tax
Holidays, conventions—$19.08 per day, including tax
Two weeks maximum stay
369 hookups, laundry and shower facilities, pool, Jacuzzi,
convenience store

Good Sam's Hitchin' Post Camper Park
3640 Las Vegas Boulevard N.
Las Vegas, NV 89115
702-644-1043
Daily (one person or married couple)—$18.36
Weekly—$108
Doesn't take reservations October through March
195 hookups, laundry and shower facilities, pool, 30- and
50-amp hookups, in-park propane delivery

KOA Kampgrounds
4315 Boulder Highway
Las Vegas, NV 89121
702-451-5527
Daily (one person or two people)—$28.57, including tax
Weekly (one person or two people)—$157.94, including tax
300 sites, laundry and shower facilities, pool, Jacuzzi, recreation room, free Strip shuttle

Several membership-only RV parks, including Hacienda Camperland RV, Sky Mountain Resort, and Thousand Trails, have Las Vegas locations.

Campers can find places to pitch their tents in the Las Vegas orbit, too. There's a free fifteen-tent site at Red Rock Canyon. Though it's difficult to find a space, if you do, you can stay for up to fourteen days. Best time to try for a spot is midday.

There are also tent sites at Mt. Charleston and at various campgrounds around Lake Mead. Some of the campgrounds are free; others may cost up to $8 per night. If you're interested in camping farther from Las Vegas, you might consider Valley of Fire, where sites cost $7 per night plus $4 park entrance fee.

An Option for Young Adventurers

If you have a hostel-association membership card or international student identification, you're welcome to stay at the Las Vegas Youth Hostel (1208 Las Vegas Boulevard S. 702-385-9955) for $13.95 a night, including tax. Accommodations are in men's and women's dorms and there's a kitchen that can be used by guests. There's no curfew at the hostel, and free coffee, tea, TV, and videos are available. However, the hostel's located on a part of the Strip where it's not considered wise to walk alone after dark.

Ship Ahoy!

Lake Mead, only twenty-five minutes away from Las Vegas, provides you with an out-of-the-ordinary lodging alternative—

renting a houseboat. Commute to the Strip when you're in the mood for glitz and glitter, laze around on the deck, swim and fish when you're not.

Though houseboat rentals don't come cheap, they become a bargain when the cost is shared by four or five couples. They're also ideal for mini-reunions or family groups who want only a taste of the excitement of Las Vegas.

Two companies on the lake rent houseboats—Seven Crown Resorts (P.O. Box 1409, Boulder City, NV, 89005, 800-752-9669) and Callville Bay Marina (Box 100 HCR-30, Las Vegas, NV 89124-9410, 800-255-5561). Located at the Lake Mead Marina, the Seven Crown Resort's houseboats that sleep ten cost $1,350 to $1,850 for seven days in summer but they're $300 less from mid-September to mid-May. During that same period (mid-September to mid-May), houseboats that sleep six cost $850 for four days and $1,250 for seven. The Callville Bay houseboat rates are divided into four groups—regular, value, spring, and fall. Weekly rates for boats that sleep ten are $1,850 during the regular season (summer), $795 during value season, $1,275 in spring, and $1,425 in fall.

4

Dining

Though I have known people who say they "eat to live," I've never quite believed them. Especially if they're talking about the food they eat on vacation. For most of us, a good part of the joy in travel is sampling the cuisine at new places or chowing down at old favorites. And it's even more fun when we leave at home that nagging voice that tells us to eat sensibly.

If, like me, you're one of those people whose vacation pleasure includes dining with abandon—not counting calories or worrying about eating balanced meals—and if you don't want to spend a heck of a lot of money on food, Las Vegas will provide a smorgasbord of options for you to try.

Now, I'm not suggesting that Las Vegas rivals New Orleans or San Francisco when it comes to the consistent high quality of its restaurants. You can—and do—get a bum meal once in a while; one that's mediocre fairly often. But that doesn't mean you can't eat well on a budget. Especially if you follow a few rules.

1. Don't assume the food is good just because the line is long at a particular buffet. Maybe four tour buses just pulled in. The best way to find out if a buffet—or any other kind of eating place—deserves raves or raspberries is by talking to people whose gastronomic judgment you trust. If you don't know anyone, ask if you can look the buffet over *before* you pay to eat there. Then use both your eyes and your nose. Watery scrambled eggs and lettuce that's brown around the

edges are dead giveaways. And good food usually smells good!

2. Be suspect of too-cheap seafood buffets. Las Vegas residents who eat out regularly say that you have to pay at least $11 or $12 to get a good-quality seafood spread. After all, seafood—even when bought in large quantities at wholesale prices—is expensive.

3. Start out the day with all-you-can-eat pancakes—or some other hearty breakfast that will stick to your ribs, since breakfast is generally the meal that gives you the most for your money. Also, carry along a snack when you go exploring. That way, you can take the time to find a coffee shop that looks good instead of settling, because you're starving, for the first one that comes along.

4. If you decide to take advantage of free hot dogs and 59¢ dinners, be prepared for paper plates, plastic utensils, and an ambience that may leave much to be desired. My solution to this situation turns adversity into advantage. Since everything's disposable, carry your food to the nearest surroundings that are pleasant—the hotel's pool area perhaps, or a bench half a block off the Strip—instead of sitting at a partially cleared table or standing at a chest-high counter in the midst of casino hubbub.

5. When you have a car, try off-the-Strip restaurants such as Poppa Gar's (1624 W. Oakey Boulevard, 702-483-4513 or 4067), an unpretentious place with home-style cooking, patronized for years by Las Vegas' power people. These restaurants that depend for business on locals give value for the prices they charge in order to keep customers coming back again and again.

6. Make lunch, which is a good deal less expensive than dinner, your main meal of the day. You'll often find that when restaurants serve the same entrées for both meals, dinner costs significantly more.

7. Just because a restaurant is reviewed in a freebie weekly mag doesn't mean it's good. It just means that the restaurant advertises in that magazine.

8. When it's free and you don't like it, don't eat it.

Sizing Up the Buffets

In the Strip's early days, the main reason lots of people visited Las Vegas wasn't for the gambling, but rather for its buffets. Those at the Hacienda fifty years ago were legendary—all you could eat for $1. And the other casinos did a creditable job, too, of competing with the Hacienda's lavish spreads.

The buffets are still a big Las Vegas draw. But except for those at the very top of the price range, as far as my palate is concerned, they're usually not that much to write home about anymore. Of course, you get a lot of food for very little money. As much as, or more than, you can eat. But instead of taking big helpings of fresh shrimp and really prime rib and gorgeous fruit salads—knowing that it will be delicious and you'll want to eat it all—you have to be a lot more selective.

The following chart will give you a rundown of what buffets currently cost at major Las Vegas properties. Prices given do not include tax. Serving hours vary fairly significantly, so it's best to check them out in advance.

Buffet	Breakfast	Lunch	Dinner	Brunch
Aladdin Hotel & Casino	$4.95	$5.95	$6.95	
Arizona Charlie's	3.50	3.95	5.50	
Bally's			11.95	7.95
Caesars Palace	7.50	7.95	13.25	
Circus Circus	2.99	3.99	4.99	
Continental Hotel	2.95	3.95	5.95	
Crab leg buffet			9.95	
Desert Inn (Champagne, Sundays)				50.00

Buffet	Breakfast	Lunch	Dinner	Brunch
Excalibur	3.99	4.99	5.99	
Fitzgerald's	4.49	4.99	6.99	
Flamingo	6.25	6.95	8.45/9.95	
Fremont (Sam Boyd's)	3.95	4.95	7.95	
Tuesday, Friday, Saturday seafood buffet			12.95	
Sunday champagne brunch				6.95
Gold Cost	2.95	4.45	6.45	
Sunday brunch (all buffets include alcoholic				
beverage)				6.45
Golden Nugget				
(Mon–Sat)	5.25	7.50	9.50	
Hacienda Hotel & Casino	2.99	3.99	5.99	
Harrah's	4.99	5.99	7.99	
Imperial Palace	4.99	5.99	6.99	
Monday–Friday brunch				5.95
Saturday–Sunday champagne brunch				6.50
Lady Luck				
Seafood buffet (Friday)	3.49	4.99	6.99	
Las Vegas Hilton	5.99	7.99	17.99	
Luxor	4.99	5.49	7.49	
Maxim Hotel			5.49/6.95	
MGM Grand	4.95	5.95	7.95	
Palace Station	3.95	5.95	7.95	
Sundays				6.95
Rio Suite Hotel & Casino	3.99	5.99	7.99	7.99
Riviera Hotel	4.95	5.95	7.95	

Buffet	Breakfast	Lunch	Dinner	Brunch
Sahara Hotel	4.95	5.95	6.95	
Sunday champagne brunch				7.95
Sam's Town (Mon–Fri)				3.95
Saturday–Sunday			6.49	5.95
Sands Hotel	5.99	4.99	9.99	
San Remo	4.95	5.95	6.95	5.95
Santa Fe Hotel & Casino	3.95	4.50	6.95	
Sunday brunch				6.95
Showboat		4.45	6.45	
Wednesday and Sunday seafood			7.45	
Saturday–Sunday brunch				5.45
Stardust (Mon–Fri)	4.95	5.95	7.95	
Saturday–Sunday champagne brunch				6.95
Tropicana (Sunday)				20.95
Westward Ho Casino	4.95	5.95	6.95	

You can subtract $1 from many of these buffet prices as discount coupons for the various spreads are generally widely distributed, although you'll get some of them only if you check into the hotels where the buffets are located.

Most of the more expensive buffets, as well as a few of the others, have children's prices. Though they cost more than most, the buffets at Caesars get high marks. A couple of dollars less, the Golden Nugget buffets have an excellent reputation with Las Vegas residents. It's clean, the surroundings are attractive, and the food is tastefully prepared. The buffets at the Rio receive a lot of praise, too. They stand out from the others because dishes are imaginative and different from the ordinary casino sirloin tips, macaroni salads, fried chicken, and creamed halibut.

Show Stopper

One buffet in Las Vegas gets standing ovations from just about everyone who has eaten of its bounty. The Sterling Brunch, presented by Bally's each Sunday from 9:30 A.M. to 2:30 P.M. for $39.95 per person.

What most people don't know is that the Sterling Brunch chefs put on a cooking school each Saturday, which costs just $15 to attend. At the demonstration, the chefs—who, incidentally, are charming and clever—prepare two of the dishes they'll serve at the next day's buffet. And participants get to eat this fancy fare after the dishes are done. Seating is limited, so you must make reservations to attend.

A Critique of Buffet Techniques

Whichever buffet you choose, you'll enjoy it more if you have planned your approach. There's nothing worse than a buffet plate piled so high that each different item gets mixed in with the ones next to, over, and under it—remember the lime-Jell-O salad that melted into the beef Stroganoff? Experts advise that you circle the buffet before you put anything on your plate. Then take small portions of the dishes you think you're going to like. Try each of them at your table, then return to the serving stations for larger helpings of the foods you particularly enjoy.

If you're really interested in getting more bite for your buck, be aware that food and beverage executives constantly have their eyes on the bottom line, even if the buffets are a casino's loss leader. They know how much each item on the buffet table costs per serving, so for every relatively high-cost dish on the menu, there will be others that cost little to produce. That means go for the prime rib, strawberries, and labor-intensive desserts, but leave the spaghetti and chocolate pudding alone.

Whatever you do, remember that while it's quite all right to take all the food you want to eat at the table, it's not acceptable to slip food into your pocket or purse for later in the day, and such action may result in an embarrassing encounter with the manager.

The Other Casino Tables

In addition to its buffets, each major casino has several other restaurants. Recently, franchise operations of national chains have been added. At the Stardust, for instance, there's a Tony Roma's (look for the coupon entitling the bearer to a free half onion loaf with the purchase of an entrée). You'll find a Burger King in the Riviera and a McDonald's in Fitzgerald's.

Among the less expensive casino restaurants, the steak house at Circus is considered a good value by Las Vegas residents. Another place you might enjoy is Ralph's Diner at the Stardust, where you can eat a Blue Plate Special ($4.95 if you have the $1-off coupon from the Stardust funbook) and drink a milk shake from the old-fashioned soda fountain, while picking out tunes from the fifties and sixties on the jukebox.

For blackened and barbecued everything, Joe's Bayou in Harrah's (702-369-5000) is a good choice. Prices are somewhat higher, but Harrah's has a reputation for consistent quality. The favorite here is the sampler—BBQ ribs, catfish, fried chicken, frog legs, and shrimp.

Casino Gourmet Dining

Food fanciers who know their béarnaises from their béchamels tell me that, for the most part, casino gourmet is an oxymoron. For, you see, the last thing hotel/casinos want to do is to intimidate their guests. So they go out of their way to make them feel at home. Dining-room (decor may combine Tivoli lights with home-on-the-range paintings; menus include such nongourmet items as turkey and dressing.

However, some Las Vegas casino gourmet rooms are really and truly gourmet. Palace Court at Caesars and Elaine's at the Golden Nugget come to mind as two of the best. The problem is, they're pricey. And though high rollers are comped, ordinary people won't usually get any discounts. But don't give up yet. If you plan to stay at one of the top hotels, be sure to ask about their room packages. Dinner for two in the gourmet restaurant may be included—or at least a free bottle of the house wine when you dine there.

Hot Dog and Hamburger Heaven

If you decide to splurge on an eating extravaganza, you can compensate for the expense at other meals, taking advantage of the food deals that most casinos offer to entice people inside. Foot-long hot dogs—free (the one at Lady Luck is outstanding) or for 99¢ (one coupon gives you the hot dog *and* a beverage for that price)—are the most common food giveaways in Las Vegas these days. The wieners are enormous; the buns, fresh. In fact, they're better than you get at most ballparks—and lots bigger. At Fiesta, you have the choice of a foot-long or a jumbo all-beef hot dog (go for the jumbo).

Hamburgers are popular giveaways, too—usually two for the price of one. The Flamingo Hilton's Food Fantasy is one of the places currently offering the twofer. Since their prices are competitive with those of hamburgers elsewhere in town, these offers are genuine specials.

Grazing as You Go

If, like me, you don't feel you have to eat proper meals when you're on vacation, you can live for days spending minimum amounts on food. Two hours after the free continental breakfast at the Westward Ho, you may decide to take advantage of the Baskin-Robbins ice cream offer at the Flamingo. A couple of boxes of free popcorn, candy samples, and free soft drinks later, it's time for Monday-night football or Tuesday-night happy hour or....

Whatever the occasion, there are always bound to be predinner specials at casino bars and lounges, where you can get your fill of pretzels or chicken wings for the price of a beer. And if you don't, there are convenience stores along the Strip and downtown where you can buy a little something to tide you over until the next freebie.

While you're grazing, you can take advantage of a fistful of coupons that give you one item of food or drink free if you buy another. They're the coupons that give you free fries or a soft drink if you buy a burger, a free piece of pizza when you buy one at the regular price, a free six-inch submarine sandwich if you buy a foot-long sub. These work best, of course, if you're really hungry or have brought along a friend.

Turn Your Night Into Day

This may sound extreme, I know. But after all, Las Vegas *is* a twenty-four-hour town. So you may find yourself going to bed at four A.M. and sleeping till noon. Having dinner at midnight. And that works out really well since some a casinos specialize in graveyard specials. They're served from ten or eleven P.M. to five or six A.M. with the hopes that, after you've eaten, you'll decide to play a few dollars at the blackjack tables or quarters in the video poker machines.

Binion's Horseshoe in Glitter Gulch is the acknowledged leader in the after-hours food department. It's reported that some locals take advantage of their 10 P.M. to 5:45 A.M. $3 New York strip-steak dinner every night. The ten-ounce steak is accompanied by a salad, baked potato, rolls, and butter. They also have a huge breakfast (eggs, ham, bacon or sausage, home-fried potatoes, toast, jelly, and coffee) that's served until two P.M.

and costs only $2.75. If you're content with two big meals a day, you could get by for just $5.75 plus tips.

Kady's Coffee Shop at the Riviera is big on graveyard specials, too. From midnight to six A.M., you can get all the flapjacks you can eat and all the coffee you can drink for $1.99; sweet and sour pork, fried rice, and eggroll for $2.99; and a ham steak and eggs breakfast at the same price.

The prize for the very cheapest casino meals, however, has to go to the Holiday Inn/Boardwalk. Throughout the year, they offer a variety of 99-cent specials, one of which is all-you-can-eat pancakes. They serve $1.29 dinners, too.

Choices, Choices

Casinos aren't directly responsible for all of Las Vegas' low-cost eating alternatives. But perhaps they are indirectly. Because the casinos—large and small—*can* afford to underwrite low-cost buffets, graveyard specials, and breakfasts at rock-bottom prices, noncasino eateries—except for the top gourmet restaurants—can't afford to charge the kinds of prices you have to pay in other metropolitan areas. And you'll usually find that even the meals in upper-end restaurants are less expensive than comparable fare in places like Manhattan and Miami Beach.

Even if you're a meat-and-potatoes person at home, Las Vegas is the place to be gastronomically adventurous. After all, if you don't care for your choice of lunch or dinner, it isn't going to cost you a mint. And if you didn't get filled up, you can always use one of those ubiquitous discount coupons and have your second meal at a buffet or fill up on free food.

It's important to keep your priorities in mind, however. If food is very important in your vacation scheme of things and you're discriminating about what you eat, you lose half of your holiday's benefit if you choose your meals solely on the basis of price and they turn out to be uninspiring. Therefore, the ultimate dining bargain is food that you enjoy eating at good-value prices. The following will give you some ideas on how to find some memorable meals.

Eat Ethnic

Time was when, although there were a handful of Italian and French restaurants in Las Vegas, it was best known for mainstream-America dishes at casino buffets. Today, things are different. The city has close to two hundred ethnic restaurants, including those that specialize in Greek, Moroccan, and Vietnamese food.

The transformation took place during the trendy eighties, when ethnic dining became popular. At the same time, Nevada's population boomed. More and more people—and restaurateurs—of diverse cultures moved to Las Vegas, adding a rich new chapter to the city's social heritage.

Just about every major hotel/casino in town has one or more restaurants where ethnic foods are served. Italian fare predominates with Bally's, Harrah's, Excalibur, MGM Grand, Riviera, Sahara, Sam's Town, Sands, and Sheraton Desert Inn— as well as restaurants in the new casinos—dishing up plates of pasta and veal piccata.

The Chinese restaurants in casinos range from the posh Empress Court at Caesars Palace with menu items like birds'-nest soup and abalone to the Emperor's Room at Lady Luck where you can get a mountain of egg rolls, chow mein, et. al. for less than $10.

At least a dozen casinos serve Mexican food, too, and Dosa Den at the Tropicana specializes in dishes such as vegetarian dosas (lentil and rice crepes with spicy potato filling) from the south of India. At the Sheraton Desert Inn, the Monte Carlo, with its French gourmet meals, falls into the splurge category.

At Yolie's Brazilian Steakhouse & Lounge (3900 Paradise Road; 702-794-0700), you might want to try *Rodizio*, which consists of a taste-tempting array of skewered meats. Whatever you order, save room for the flan or bananas in caramel sauce.

For decades there have been Mexican restaurants in Las Vegas, but their number increased dramatically in the eighties when Nevada's Hispanic population grew from about 54,000 to 124,000. Eating Mexican in Las Vegas today requires some hard choices, since more than three dozen restaurants serve enchiladas, flautas, and the like. Among my favorites is Macayo Vegas (1741 E. Charleston Boulevard, 702-382-5606), which has been around for about thirty-five years. Decor is cheerful, but not cutesy. And though the menu choices are typical, the food is especially well prepared (try the beef fajitas).

Another Mexican restaurant favored by the locals is Garcia's (1030 E. Flamingo Road, 702-731-0628) where specialties include chimichangas and Mexican pizza—a flour tortilla topped with cheese and spicy beef, salsa, and diced tomatoes. Garcia's frequently puts out coupons, such as a two-for-one fajita deal. Chapala (3335 E. Tropicana, 702-451-8141) is popular with residents, too.

If you like Mexican dishes, why not expand your culinary experiences with other Latin flavors. La Casa Cuba (2501 E. Tropicana, 702-454-6310) specializes in authentic dishes like *paella Valenciana* and *tasajo con arroz y frijoles* (shredded beef, rice, and black beans with a special blend of Cuban spices). Salvadoreno (720 N. Main Street, 702-385-3600) is not in the best of neighborhoods and the decor isn't much either, but the food is another story. *Pupusas* (tortillas filled with cheese), *pollo encebollado* (chicken with onions), and *carne guisada* (beef stew) are among the inexpensive house specialties.

During the eighties, people from the Pacific Rim and Southeast Asian countries began pouring into Las Vegas. To the already established Chinese and Japanese restaurants, Vietnamese, Filipino, Thai, and East Indian cafes added more flavors of the Far East. Many of these restaurants offer complete meals in the $5-to-$10 price range—and provide out-of-the-ordinary dining experiences in the bargain.

Ghandi (4080 Paradise at Flamingo , 702-734-0094) features dishes from five different regions of India in a setting of East

Indian elegance (ask to be seated on the balcony). Specialty dishes include *tandoori* chicken, which is marinated and cooked in a clay oven; *raita,* a cucumber and yogurt salad, and the East Indian bread called *naan.* Look for the $5-off coupon dinner for two.

Thai Spice Restaurant (4433 W. Flamingo Road, 702-362-5308) features ten daily lunch specials priced at $4.95. Pepper garlic pork, *moo goo gai pan* (chicken stir-fry with vegetables), and mint-leaf chicken are among the choices, which you can have spiced to your taste on a scale of one to ten. Ten is *very, very* hot. At the Vietnamese restaurant A Touch of Ginger (4110 S. Maryland Parkway, 702-796-1770), the house special is—appropriately—ginger beef.

As far as Chinese restaurants go, Chin's (3200 Las Vegas Boulevard S., 702-733-8899) is definitely a cut above all others. Located in Fashion Show Mall, it's right in the middle of the action on the strip. So can you afford it? You certainly can, if you have lunch, which is a good deal less expensive than dinner, as your main meal that day. You'll dine in an atmosphere of understated elegance on such lunch specials ($8.95) as summer noodle salad, a mélange of julienne of chicken, cucumber, and bean sprouts atop warm noodles and served with a peanut sesame dressing. The specials include the soup of the day.

Among the Japanese restaurants, the charming Ginza (1000 E. Sahara Avenue, 702-732-3080) is a favorite with locals. House specialty is *yosenabe,* a fish stew of clams, crab, fish, and shrimp, which is said to be the Japanese version of *bouillabaisse*. At another recommendable restaurant, Tokyo (Commercial Center Shopping Plaza, 953 E. Sahara, 702-735-7070), you can cook your own skewered beef, chicken, seafood, and vegetables on tabletop hibachis. Dinners also include soup, pickles, rice, dessert, and green tea.

There are also European, North African, and Middle Eastern restaurants in abundance where you can find quality meals at reasonable prices.

Alpine Village Inn (3003 Paradise Road, across from the

Convention Center) may cost a little more, but you're paying for atmosphere, too. The ambience is that of a mountain hamlet with snow and twinkling lights. The food servers wear dirndls and lederhosen, and meals are old-country German down to the pumpernickel bread, *Wiener schnitzel* and *wurst*. There's also a *rathskeller,* where meals are less formal and less expensive.

Nippon (101 Convention Center; 702-735-5565) features a *shabu-shabu* bar where diners cook their own veggies, noodles and steak, chicken or seafood. If you want someone else to do the work, opt for the sushi bar.

At Battista's Hole in the Wall (one-quarter mile east of the Strip off Flamingo at 4041 Audrie, 702-732-1424), you can eat your pasta, veal piccante, and other Italian dishes in a casual, Old World atmosphere that's lots of fun. Among the menu selections are homemade manicotti and fettuccine with meatballs, sausage, or seafood. And the lineup of veal entrées is impressive—it's prepared alla bolognese, marsala, milanese, parmigiana, and piccante. Dining at Battista's is not cheap, but the dinner price does include wine and a cup of cappuccino.

Dinners at country-French Pamplemousse, in an old house at 400 E. Sahara (702-733-2066), start with a big basket of fresh vegetables and go on to such delicacies as Norwegian salmon with orange curry sauce and Wisconsin duckling with green peppercorns. Dinners start at $16, very reasonable as far as French restaurants are concerned. And the food is wonderful.

The family-owned Olympic Cafe & Restaurant (4029 Spring Mountain Road, 702-876-7900) is another of Las Vegas' gastronomic institutions that have been around for a while. Gyro beef-lamb sandwiches, *moussaka* (eggplant), *spanakopita* (spinach pie), and *dolmathes* (stuffed grape leaves) are only a few of the Greek dishes on the menu.

At Mamounia (4632 S. Maryland Parkway, 702-736-7655) diners sit on pillows at low, highly decorated tables. Waiters wear caftans and slippers. There are belly dancers, too. Traditional North African dishes arrive in a seven-course dinner, which includes *pastilla* (ground chicken, almonds, and scrambled eggs topped with *phyllo* dough), a flaming lamb brochette, and an extremely sweet dessert called *chabakia*. Though prices are in the splurge category, the experience is memorable. Be prepared to eat with your hands.

To get back on an even economic keel, you might eat at Mediterranean Cafe & Market (4147 S. Maryland Parkway, 702-731-6030) where the house specialty is the kabob sandwich. Other items on the menu include gyros salad, hummus, tabbouleh, Middle Eastern coffees (including Turkish), and an unusual homemade ice cream that contains rose water, saffron, and pistachio nuts. You place your order at the back of the grocery store.

Local Favorites

Like the ethnic restaurants, many of the following don't fall into the discount-coupon category, and some of them aren't necessarily considered cheap places to eat. But they are a sampling of Las Vegas restaurants that offer good value for money spent.

Holy Cow! (2423 Las Vegas Boulevard S., 702-732-2697) is the most conveniently located for tourists of the four restaurants in Big Dog's Hospitality Group. Take your beer sampler from either the one o'clock or five o'clock brewery tour (see chapter 5, "Attractions and Entertainment,") to the restaurant and order either lunch or dinner. The menu includes a good selection of bratwurst (served on a bun with fries and coleslaw) starting at $3.85, and entrées such as fish 'n' chips and rotisserie herb chicken, both at $6.95. Another good bet is Joe's Special—a combination of ground beef. spinach, sautéed onions, and scrambled eggs—listed as a breakfast item, but served with home fries all day long ($3.95).

Harrie's Bagelmania (855 E. Twain Avenue, 702-369-3322) sells about 150 dozen bagels a day, ranging from such standards as egg and pumpernickel to the more unusual jalapeño-cheese and combination bagel (an everything-but-the-kitchen-sink affair that is Harrie's bestseller. They also make wonderful *bialys,* sort of a cross between a bagel and an English muffin.

If you know what's good for you, you'll want to have lunch at Wild Oats Community Market (6720 W. Sahara; 702-253-7050). Shakes made with nonfat frozen yogurt and skim milk, vegetarian pasta with wheat balls, and all sorts of imaginative sandwiches will convince you that healthful foods are anything but ho-hum.

Country Inn (2425 E. Desert Inn Road, 702-731-5035) is yet another local favorite. And the prices are definitely in the no-pain zone. The chicken-fried steak sells for $4.50 and the turkey steak favorite for $4.95. Banana cream and coconut cream pies are the desserts of choice.

Though its neighborhood isn't one you would get out of your car and walk around in, Wimpy's (2437 Las Vegas Boulevard N., 702-642-5710) is a Las Vegas landmark. Food is typical drive-in-of-the-fifties-fare—hamburgers, chili dogs, banana splits, and milk shakes.

Early-Bird Specials

Just as hotel/casinos have days of the week and seasons when room rates are lower, some restaurants offer special prices at certain times of the day and/or year. These specials may be advertised in newspapers and the weekly magazines. More likely, they're only advertised on signs outside the restaurants. Usually, the only meal with price differentials is dinner. You may find that you can afford to dine in a restaurant that's ordinarily out of your price range. For example, Phillip's Supper House (4545 E. Sahara Avenue, 702-873-5222) recently served their $18.95 steak dinner for $13.95 if it was ordered between five P.M. and 6 P.M. The Venetian (3713 W. Sahara Avenue, 702-876-4190) is another somewhat expensive restaurant where early-bird specials make a big economic difference.

Pack a Picnic

Most months of the year, Las Vegas weather is ideal for eating outdoors. There are picnic tables and grills at most of the area's sightseeing spots, such as Red Rock Canyon and Lake Mead. In the city itself, you'll find outdoor eating facilities at the major parks. Among the nicest are Sunset Park (2575 E. Sunset Road) and Floyd Lamb State Park on the north edge of the city, which has been a favorite with Las Vegas families for years.

The supermarket closest to the Strip—Myer's Market (22 E. Oakey Boulevard)—carries a complete stock of groceries as well as paper picnic products and briquettes. To get to Myer's, take one of the Strip–downtown buses to the first stop north of Vegas World, get off, and walk west a few hundred feet.

Breakfast at a Bakery

Freed's (4780 S. Eastern Avenue, 702-456-7762) isn't a gussied-up bakery by any means. There's little pretense at decor—stacks of plastic-windowed boxes containing wedding-cake decorations on the shelves; a couple of Formica tables and chairs for customers who can't wait to get outside to eat their goodies. But it's Las Vegas' oldest bakery and most residents I've talked to say it is where they buy their baked goods. And anyway, who needs ambience when such delights as Hungarian cheesecake (my favorite), poppy seed *strudel*, French pastries, and the honey-pecan bars known as *Bienenstich* are just a point of the finger away?

Two other bakeries I like are the bakery at the new Chinatown Plaza and Albina's Italian and American Bakery (30–35 E. Tropicana, Suite A-2, 702-433-5400). At the Chinatown Plaza bakery, (4255 Spring Mountain Road; 702-221-8448) counters brim with such delights as kiwi mango and peach mousse cakes, coconut bread, red bean toast, and a variety of buns (try the lotus buns for breakfast; the onion and bacon if it's lunchtime). An added treat is the display of wedding cakes and cake decorations near the entrance. Albina's specialties incude such Italian favorites as *cannoli, cassatine, pasticciotti,* and *sfogliatella.*

If you're diabetic, you can still have a baked-goods breakfast since Mrs. Williams Diabetic Delights (3466 S. Decatur Boulevard, 702-362-1243) produces more than two dozen kinds of pies, cakes, coffee cakes, muffins, and cookies. Tip: try the cherry coffee cake.

Festival and Church-Supper Fare

You'll have to scan the newspapers or watch the community bulletin boards on TV to find out about ethnic festivals and suppers sponsored by various churches and other organizations. But they're well worth the effort. First of all, you'll get to sample homemade specialties you might not otherwise get to try, and secondly, they're almost always reasonably priced, and in some cases, a portion of the price is tax deductible.

Supermarket Sample Days

If you're really low on funds, but have a set of wheels, you can get filled up eating supermarket samples—cottage cheese, turkey salami, prepackaged pasta dishes, ice cream, crackers with spreads of all kinds. The two big chains, Vons and Lucky, have their sample days on Friday and Saturday afternoons, but not every week. If you have a Costco card, you'll be able to sample the samples most any day of the week.

Bon appétit!

5

♠

Attractions and Entertainment

You can spend a fortune keeping yourself entertained in Las Vegas. No doubt about that. It's also possible to get by spending next to nothing. But I'll bet one of the reasons you decided to visit Vegas was to see a show or two. And it would be a pity to miss out on attractions you would really like to see just because there's an admission charge.

So, this chapter is about having it all—or at least most of it—as cheaply as possible. Taking into account, of course, that having it all doesn't necessarily mean the same thing to every one of us.

Obviously, space won't permit us to tell you about every single thing there is to see and do in Las Vegas. Therefore, the attractions and entertainments highlighted in this chapter have been selected on the basis of our opinion of what's good value for money spent, and an acknowledged element of subjectivity.

I realize, however, that we're all coming from different places, literally and figuratively. While you may adore bungee jumping, I wouldn't try it except on pain of death. So I have reluctantly included it as a sport, one you won't be doing with my blessing. And though I love ballet, maybe you don't. So read around the activities that you're not interested in and concentrate on those you are.

Starting Point

Since the premise of this book is to maximize your Las Vegas vacation dollars, you'll need to start your stay with a coupon-collecting expedition, if you haven't acquired a slew of them by mail before leaving home. Grab every free weekly events magazine, such as *Tourguide* and *Las Vegas Today*, plus promotional material from individual casinos that you can get your hands on.

You'll find these giveaway cards, brochures, and magazines at car rental agencies, hotels, the airport, and tourist stations on the Strip (for a complete listing of places to look, see chapter 12, "Sources and Resources"). If you have time for only two stops, go to the Las Vegas Convention Center tourist office, just to the right of the main door, and to the Las Vegas Chamber of Commerce, which is a couple of long blocks away at 711 E. Desert Inn Road.

When you've collected your wad, take time to clip out and sort through the coupons. Divide them into categories—food and drink, admissions, gaming, shopping discounts, free souvenirs—and throw out those that you're positive you'll never use. Then put on your sensible shoes, grab your coupons (fanny packs are convenient to carry them in), and get ready to go.

Strip Stroll/Casino Crawl

The casinos are—needless to say—the magnet that draws most people to Las Vegas. So they're the places you most likely will want to visit first.

Exploring every casino on the Strip thoroughly could take weeks, so we've devised three tours, which will allow you to do the Strip in three segments, hitting the high spots and a few in between. Each of the three tours should take about two and a half to three hours. If you decide to combine the tour with a coupon crawl—redeeming the gaming coupons you've decided are worthwhile—it may take longer.

Tour One, South Strip:

The Luxor, one of Las Vegas' newest hotel/casinos is the starting point for this tour. Its pyramidal shape and giant cats guarding the entrance look impressive from the air, but slightly hokey from ground's-eye view. Nonetheless, the interior decor of the casino—in shades of orange, blue, and gold—sets it apart from other casinos, and that to my mind is a real plus.

The three interactive experiences at Luxor are novel, rather expensive ($5 for one, $4 for each of the others), and can be confusing if you don't watch the explanatory video first, then take them in sequence—"In Search of the Obelisk" first, followed by "Luxor Live" and "The Theater of Time." To participate in the latter, you climb into one of the passenger "sleds" whose motion coincides with that on the 180-degree, 25-foot screen. Each of the experiences lasts four and a half minutes.

From Luxor, take the monorail to its next-door neighbor, Excalibur. Unless you have youngsters along or are mad for carnival games, you'll want to skip the lower level, with its "dungeon" arcade and Magic Motion Simulator thrill ride. You will probably enjoy your time more by poking around the Medieval Village, with its shops, restaurants, and concessions on the second floor.

Entertainers in medieval costumes—jugglers, musicians, mimes—stroll the walkways. Caricaturists sketch their subjects. And at an especially entertaining concession, photographers transfer customers' faces on to magazine covers. While you're watching the photographers at work, you can see via closed-circuit television how the finished products are going to look.

Each night King Arthur and his court preside over dinner shows featuring Merlin the magician and mounted knights of the Round Table, who take part in a jousting tournament. And don't be surprised while you are at Excalibur to see a wedding party in full medieval garb coming out of the Canterbury Wedding Chapel. After all, you're in Las Vegas.

Across the Strip to the east, exotic butterflies flutter about and Amazon parrots preen their feathers at Tropicana's Wildlife Walk, the new bird and wildlife habitat situated on the covered walkway linking the hotel's two towers. Pygmy marmosets— the world's smallest monkeys—moluccan cockatoos, toucans, flamingos, African crowned cranes arid schools of koi fish are among the habitat's other residents.

North of the Tropicana and across the street stands MGM Grand Hotel, Casino & Theme Park, Las Vegas' newest and the largest hotel in the world. Though biggest isn't necessarily best, it surely attracts attention. When the MGM Grand's second incarnation (the first MGM Grand is now Bally's) was unveiled in mid-December 1993, network TV, journalists for national and international newspapers, and hundreds of VIPs were in attendance.

After entering the MGM's main entrance (you come in through the lion's mouth), you'll be in Emerald City, with its Oz Buffet, Emerald City Casino, Monkey Bar, and seven-story Casablanca Tower. Continuing on through variously named casino areas and a variety of coffee shops and restaurants, you finally arrive at the theme park entrance (described in chapter 10, "Family Fun"). Incredible as it may seem, the place is a mile long from lion's mouth to the tail end of the theme park.

North of MGM Grand, the Aladdin is an Arabian-themed hotel/casino that might look familiar even though you've never visited it before as it's a favorite with TV and movie directors for shooting casino scenes. While looking around, if you feel a sudden need for another funbook, you can pick one up at the casino cage. And though you may think it's just so much hype, it's a fact. Elvis *was* married at the Aladdin.

Not far north of the Aladdin at Don Pablo Cigar Company (3025 Las Vegas Boulevard S.), you can watch four Cuban master cigar makers who roll about a thousand of the stogies each day. They use tobacco from five different countries, and if you're in a buying mood, there's a coupon available in freebie magazines for $5 off per box.

Continuing north, you might want to stop for a banana split at the charming ice cream parlor in the shopping arcade of Bally's Hotel. Built as the MGM Grand in 1973, the hotel/casino was bought in 1986 by Bally's (a gambling-machine manufacturer). The hotel was equipped with a sprinkler system and other safety devices after the disastrous MGM fire in 1981, but still retains the original MGM Hollywood theme, with glamour photos of yesteryear's stars and other movieland memorabilia.

This is the logical place to end Tour One and take a bus back to your hotel if you are tired. People with more time and stamina may want to go on to Tour Two, Central Strip.

Across the street, north of Bally's, Barbary Coast's stained-glass murals—a clipper ship with sails billowing behind the bar and supersize enchanted forest covering an entire wall—are definitely worth stepping inside to see.

Next hotel/casino, the flamboyant Flamingo Hilton, gives away the best casino funbook in town, Many of the coupons are redeemable at O'Shea's, the Hilton-run club next door, where you may want to stop to redeem them.

The antique-car collection at the Imperial Palace (described later in this chapter) deserves more than a quick look, so you'll probably want to visit it later, though it's the next point of interest on Tour Two.

Between the Imperial Palace and Harrah's, a cobblestone street bordered by New Orleans–style buildings with wrought-iron balconies is the perfect place to relax and listen to Dixieland music floating on the air.

Whether you stop in Harrah's, Casino Royale, and Sands Hotel/Casino on your way to the tour's turnaround point at the end of the block depends primarily on what coupons you have in your wad.

In the distance is the Sheraton Desert Inn, understatedly posh and out of the bargain category. Unless you want to examine the luxury resort at close range, cross the street to Treasure Island, where the most interesting part of this tour begins. In fact, if you become weary of casinos at the end of

Tour One, just do the segment of Tour Two that follows.

Time your arrival at Treasure Island to coincide with the naval battle of HMS *Britannia* against the pirate ship *Hispañola*. The waterside tables on the terrace of the Battle Bar are the best spot to watch it from. Wander through the pirate-themed casino, with its murals of buccaneers and buried treasure, to the tram that will take you next door to Mirage if your feet are tired. However, the best way to approach Mirage is by way of the front sidewalk.

Considered the most outstanding property on the Strip by many casino connoisseurs, Mirage's palm trees sway, waterfalls splash into a tropical lagoon, and the gilded pineapples topping the railings near the hotel/casino's entrance extend the universal symbol of welcome. Inside, the lush foliage continues, creating a junglelike ambience. Many of the plants are labeled, so you can increase your botanical knowledge as you stroll.

Near the south entrance of Mirage, you can watch rare royal white tigers doze, prowl, and play in a glass-fronted habitat. This species of snow-white tiger, which comes from the Himalayas, is now extinct in the wild, but they seem to thrive under the care of illusionists Siegfried and Roy, in whose show at the Mirage they appear—and disappear.

While the tiger habitat is a free attraction, the Mirage's dolphin habitat is not. For $3 (children under three are admitted free), you can take a short guided tour of the special marine facility, which contains more than a one million gallons of man-made seawater and five adult bottlenose dolphins. Located in the pool area of the hotel, the fascinating sea mammals can be viewed from both above and below water level from nine A.M. to seven P.M. on weekends and from eleven A.M. to seven P.M. weekdays.

If you're like most tourists, you'll want to revisit the Mirage at night when the volcano erupts every fifteen minutes after dark.

Chances are, you'll have a pretty strong opinion about Caesars Palace, next property on the Strip. Either that it's too corny/gauche or really neat. True, the statuary—Roman states-men, philosophers, poets, a charioteer, and an incongruous Joe Louis—is ostentatious in the extreme. And the stately voice heralding the wonders inside (with a backdrop of *Quo Vadis*-like music) as visitors are transported to the entrance on a moving sidewalk is a bit much. But to my mind the place is so overthemed that somehow it works. Inside, toga-clad waitresses serve drinks, and you'll see centurions going about their various duties.

An extension of Caesars—the Forum Shops—offers a con-tinuation of the Roman theme via storefront facades, fountains, and more statues. Shops and restaurants are definitely upscale, but a trip to Las Vegas isn't complete without seeing what they look like.

Another element of Caesars, which seems incongruous theme-wise, actually fits into the theme of what the Strip is all about—luck. Located on the north lawn, it's an authentic replica of Thailand's popular Brahma shrine—one associated with good fortune and prosperity.

Tours One and Two should about do you in for one day. Since Tour Three can be combined easily with a walk around downtown, why not save it for later. The tour of the North Strip begins at Fashion Show Mall (described also in chapter 6, "Shopping.")

One of the most interesting shops in the mall for browsing is the Antiques Emporium, where you'll see jukeboxes, Coke machines, and kitchen gadgets from the forties and fifties as well as memorabilia from earlier decades. Another great place for looking around is Gifts of the World, with its wildly eclectic array, which includes a life-size merry-go-round lion and a stuffed rattlesnake.

Proceeding north, you'll pass by the western-themed Fron-tier, the Stardust, and Westward Ho. Again, whether you go inside will depend on whether you have coupons to redeem, are thirsty, or just want to sit down for a while.

If you're hungry for free popcorn or want to buy a Heineken

for just 75¢, pop into Slots-A-Fun, a small casino that's owned by Circus Circus and is next on the route. With the right coupon, you can also get a free cap there.

Be sure to stop at Circus Circus, the next casino on the Strip (described in chapter 10, "Family Fun"), if you like to watch aerialists, magicians, and the like. And though kids seem to like the Guinness Book of Records Museum (2789 Las Vegas Boulevard S.) best, adults who go for graphically illustrated trivia may find it worth the $4.95 admission ($3.95 for seniors, students, and military; $2.95 for children twelve and under). A coupon for $1 off the adult price is widely distributed.

Cross the Strip next to the Riviera, which before the advent of the MGM Grand boasted the largest casino in town. After-noons and evenings, there's lots of free entertainment at the Riv, both inside on a couple of different stages near the 21 tables and on the sidewalk outside—comics, celebrity look-alikes, mimes, and musicians. Best values in the casino's funbook are the discounts that take $3 to $5 off the admission to each of the club's four different shows.

The tourist information station south of the Riviera is a good coupon source, and beyond that the Silver City Casino is another place to get a bag of free popcorn. You also might want to spend a few minutes gazing at the Silver City's mural-covered ceiling, from which dangle all sorts of western artifacts—ore cars, pickaxes, and the like—as well as mannequins dressed as prospectors and cowboys.

One of the newest freebie attractions on the stretch of Las Vegas Boulevard north of the Strip is the Holy Cow! Free Beer Tasting & Tour. You'll probably start chuckling when you see the outside of the place. It's painted, columns and all, with black-and-white holstein spots. The motif continues inside the small casino/restaurant/"cowllectibles" gift shop, making Holy Cow! one of the most refreshing places on the boulevard. After the free tour, you'll be given a four-ounce sampler of one of the microbrewery's four handmade beers. If you've got one of their mug-shaped coupons with a cow wearing sunglasses on it, you'll also receive 10 percent off any menu item and any "cowllectible." The four beers currently produced by Las Vegas' first microbrewery are called Amber Gambler Pale Ale, Rebel Red Ale, Vegas Gold Wheat Beer, and a Brewmaster Special, which depends on the season and the brewmaster's whim. Tours are conducted on odd-numbered hours from one to five P.M.

Downtown: The Lights are Brighter There

Even if you've walked through enough casinos to last you a lifetime on your Strip stroll, you must go to Glitter Gulch, the city's downtown gambling area where it all began. The best time to see it in all its neon glory is after dark. And yes, it is true. The lights are brighter there. So bright, in fact, that you really can read a newspaper outside at midnight.

Several of the casinos are pretty seedy, with characters that look as if they've stepped from the pages of a Damon Runyon story. However, at least two of the casinos—the Golden Nugget and the Four Queens—rival most of the gambling palaces on the Strip. The Golden Nugget's public rooms are far more elegant than most, and Four Queens has become nationally known for its "Monday Night Jazz," broadcast on more than 140 radio stations across the country and abroad. Three shows on that night of the week, which feature such top-drawer musicians as Dave McKenna, are among Las Vegas' best bargains. At 7:30, 9:30, and 11:30 P.M., admission is only a two-drink minimum.

If you're a sports fan, you won't want to miss the Sports Hall of Fame at the Las Vegas Club Hotel/Casino with its baseball collection that's second only to the one at the Baseball Hall of Fame in Cooperstown, New York.

While you're downtown, be sure to have your free photo postcard taken with a backdrop of a million dollars at the Binion's Horseshoe Club, and to redeem your coupon for a free all-beef, foot-long hot dog at Lady Luck (it's worth the rather dreary walk to the back of the casino to get it). You can have a free color photo taken there, too, and make a free two-minute phone call to anywhere in the U.S.

You can get either a free watch or coffee mug at Fitzgerald's too, and restock your supply of freebie magazines at the bell desk. You'll find that Glitter Gulch casinos are usually more generous with their giveaways than Strip casinos. Since in most people's minds the Strip is Gaming Area #1, Gaming Area #2 tries harder. (See chapter 4, "Dining," for some examples of great Glitter Gulch meal deals.)

Beyond the Brighter Lights

There are yet more casinos beyond the dazzle of Glitter Gulch and the excitement of the Strip. The Showboat (2800 E. Fremont Street) is a favorite with locals, and for bowling tournaments. Out Boulder Highway, Sam's Town is a western-themed hotel/casino with an extensive collection of Coca-Cola memorabilia in its Calamity Jane's Ice Cream House.

Arizona Charlie's, on the west side of town, is another favorite with Las Vegas residents. Closer in, the Brazilian-themed Rio, Las Vegas Hilton, the San Remo, and Debbie Reynolds's Hollywood Hotel are within easy walking distance of the Strip.

If you never venture beyond Glitter Gulch and the Strip, you can't really say you've seen all that Las Vegas has to offer. So why not visit a few Las Vegas museums. Some of them are even popular with people who say they're not the museum type.

Candelabra and Sequins

Whether you were a fan of the late Liberace or you're just crazy about kitsch, you won't want to miss the Liberace Museum at 1775 E. Tropicana Avenue—even if it does cost $6.50 for adults, $4.50 for seniors, and $2 for children under twelve (you'll find two-for-one-admission coupons in some freebie magazines).

Three exhibit areas chronicle "Mr. Showmanship's" glittering career. The main museum houses the Piano, Car, and Celebrity Galleries. The Costume and Jewelry Galleries as well as re-creations of Liberace's office and bedroom from his Palm Springs hacienda, The Cloisters, are located in the Annex. The Library displays the entertainer's miniature-piano collection—one of them's made from thousands of toothpicks—and a photo history of his life and family.

One customized auto in the Car Gallery is covered with rhinestones. A one-of-a-kind Rolls-Royce glistens with thousands of mirror tiles. More mirror tiles sparkle on Liberace's favorite Baldwin grand in the Piano Gallery, while jewels, feathers, satin, and fur add to the flamboyance of his on-stage wardrobe displayed on mannequins and hangers in the Costume Gallery.

The collection is eclectic, to say the least, with several hundred pieces of rare Moser crystal from Czechoslovakia, a set of dinnerware formerly owned by John F. Kennedy, an inlaid crucifix presented to Liberace by Pope Pius XII, and his candelabrum ring with platinum candlesticks and diamond flames among the memorabilia on display. The museum is open Monday–Saturday, ten A.M. to five p.m.; Sunday, one p.m. to five P.M. A new toy or food item serves as admission on one day in early December, when the museum hosts a two-hour Christmas party with free cookies and cider. Bus No. 201.

Seeing Stars' Cars

People who are intrigued by the cars of the rich, famous, and infamous—past and present—will want to visit the Imperial Palace Auto Collection in the Imperial Palace. Located on the fifth floor of the hotel/casino's parking garage, this assemblage of important vehicles includes the King of Siam's 1928 Delage, Pope Paul VI's 1966 Chrysler Imperial, Adolf Hitler's 1939 Mercedes-Benz, Juan Perón's 1939 straight-8 Packard, and Al Capone's 1930 V-16 Cadillac.

Among the showbiz wheels on display, favorites include

W.C. Fields's 1938 Cadillac, Tom Mix's 1937 Cord, and motorcycles owned by Steve McQueen, Clark Gable, and Sammy Davis, Jr.

There are cars that made automotive history, too, such as a 1910 Thomas Flyer and the largest array of Model J Duesenbergs in the world. Although the collection has grown to more than 750 antique, classic, and special-interest vehicles, only 200 of them are on display at any one time.

Though admission to the auto collection is $6.95 for adults ($3 for seniors and children under twelve), we were able to find free-admission coupons in weekly magazines. At Las Vegas museums where admission is charged, there's almost always a way to get in at a discount. Therefore, it's a good idea to telephone in advance and ask if there are any special deals currently being offered. That way, you can also make certain that the museum will be open when you plan to visit (some of them close for a few days when mounting a special exhibit).

More Museum Hopping

At the Las Vegas Art Museum (6130 W. Charleston Avenue; 702-259-4458; bus #206) a different artist's work is featured each month and a meet-the-artist reception is held on the first Sunday. The museum's hours are Tuesday through Saturday, 10 A.M.–3 P.M. and Sunday, 12–3 P.M. Since the museum is at present in temporary quarters, its permanent collection, which includes a lithograph by Alexander Calder and a sculpture by Mauro Possobon, is on display at the Las Vegas Community College.

Though the focus at the Nevada State Museum and Historical Society at Lorenzi Park (700 Twin Lakes Drive; 702-486-5205; bus 106 or 208) is on the anthropology and natural history of southern Nevada, with emphasis on the prehistoric animals and humans who lived there, you'll also see displays of more contemporary subjects, such as the uses of neon lighting in Las Vegas. Recent exhibits have included

"Venomous Reptiles of Southern Nevada," "World War II and the Emergence of Modern Las Vegas," and "A Common Thread," which encompassed fiber arts such as wall hangings, traditional and contemporary baskets, saddle blankets, handmade paper, dolls, and awnings.

The State Museum's hours are 11:30 A.M. to 4:30 P.M. Monday and Tuesday; 8:30 A.M. to 4:30 P.M. Wednesday through Sunday. Entrance fees are $2 for adults; people under eighteen, free.

The Marjorie Barrick Museum of Natural History (702-739-3381), located on the campus of the University of Nevada, Las Vegas (UNLV), focuses on live desert reptiles, mammals, insects, archaeology, and anthropology of the Southwest. Open 9 A.M. to 5 P.M., Monday through Friday, 10 A.M. to 5 P.M., Saturday, the museum is free. Bus 109 goes to the UNLV campus.

For even more exhibits, go to the Las Vegas Library (833 Las Vegas Boulevard N., 702-382-3493, bus 113) and various community centers around town—where you'll find such displays as unusual Christmas ornaments and architect-designed dollhouses that were finalists in an international competition.

Be a Star—Or Maybe an Extra?

Las Vegas glitter, the surrounding Old West countryside, and accessibility to Los Angeles make the area a natural shooting ground for films and TV productions. The Nevada Motion Picture Division's Event Hotline (702-486-2727) tells when and where movies are currently being shot and what companies are in charge of casting them. If you're in town long enough, you may want to try out or watch the action at the shooting site.

Annual and Special Events

Las Vegas has been described as having the impact of a Wild West show and the sophistication of Monte Carlo. I'm skeptical about the sophistication claim. If you go along with Webster's definition—being deprived of genuineness, naturalness, or simplicity, made worldly-wise—Las Vegas is a lot more sophisticated than Monte Carlo ever thought of being. But go to any of the city's special events and you'll understand the Wild West show comparison.

Most of these events have a nominal admission charge. Some cost absolutely nothing. Almost all of them have an element of western hospitality and enthusiasm that's typically Las Vegas.

Many of the annual events are ethnic-themed. For instance in March, the St. Patrick's Day parade struts, rolls, and high-steps its way through downtown.

The annual feast of San Gennaro, held in late August and early September, focuses on Italian food, such as homemade pasta, sausage and peppers, and even strawberry pizza, dancing games, celebrity guests, and continuous professional entertainment. Held from six P.M. to midnight behind Bally's, admission is $4 for adults, $2 for seniors and students. Children under the age of twelve are admitted free.

At the Clark County Basque Festival in September, the descendants of people from the Pyrenees eat chorizo sausages on buns and Basco beans, drink Picon punches, dance to old-country accordion music, and compete in games (actually they're feats of strength involving chopping giant logs and carrying horrendously heavy weights). Spectators are welcome and will enjoy the eating and drinking as much as the Basques—but be aware that Picon punch is potent.

Also in September there's an annual salute to Mexican Independence Day, with piñatas, carnival games, Mexican music and food. During the same month Ho'olaule'a Pacific Islands Festival honors Hawaiian and Pacific islanders at Lorenzi Park. There's continuous music and dance entertainment from eleven A.M. to six P.M., plus fashion boutiques, arts and crafts exhibits, and food booths.

October brings Las Vegas Indian Days, which are held at the

Southern Nevada Community College in conjunction with the North Las Vegas Fairshow. A powwow, Indian music, dancing, storytelling, and arts and crafts are all part of the celebration.

And More Events

Churches also offer some interesting activities to which the public is invited via radio and TV community calendars and notices and ads in the local papers. For example, occasional masses are performed in Polish at one of the Catholic churches, and at least two synagogues put on Hanukkah parties open to the public for a small admission fee.

Community, fraternal, and business organizations put on events, too. For example, in September there's the annual KNPR Craftswork Market, sponsored by public radio. Free jazz concerts are performed by professional Strip hotel/casino musicians (Charleston Heights Art Center, 702-229-6383) at various venues throughout the year, and an annual "Search for Talent" is sponsored by the Las Vegas Breakfast Exchange club and the city.

If you're going to be downtown during a weekday noon hour, you might check to see if any brown-bag concerts are taking place that day. If you're in luck, it may be one of the free noontime concerts at the Clark County Commission Chambers by such groups as the talented Sierra Wind Quintet, which, incidentally, has also played at Carnegie Hall.

Whatever the entertainment, you'll find it's a lot better than you expected, whether an amateur theater production or a city band concert. That's because many of the talented entertainers who perform in productions on the Strip and in Glitter Gulch get bored of dancing the same routines night after night, singing the same songs, or playing the same tunes. So, to stay creatively happy, they become a part of amateur or semipro groups that perform on a less regular basis, often for free.

There are chili cook-offs, cat shows, and craft festivals

galore. Hundreds of dancers do-si-do each March at the Hoover Dam Square Dance Festival. At the October Fairshow in North Las Vegas, one hundred pilots from around the world guide their balloons skyward to provide an unforgettable spectacle that's free to anyone who looks up. Helldorado in May and the National Finals Rodeo in December offer cowboy riding at its best.

One of the funniest annual events is November's Strut Your Mutt at Dog Fancier's Park (5800 E. Flamingo Road, 702-455-8238; bus 202) when canines of all shapes, sizes, and breeds are entered in wacky contests.

The Ultimate Entertainment

If you're not already wed, you might consider getting married in Las Vegas. After all, that's pretty entertaining, and a *lot* cheaper than getting married at home where you'd have to invite a cast of thousands.

In Nevada, all you have to do is pay your $35 license fee, show proof that you're over eighteen years of age, bring along (or rent) a couple of witnesses, and find someone to marry you. The latter two—rental witnesses and a Marryin' Sam—can be had starting at about $45 (it's customary to tip the person who performs the ceremony $25 to $50, too) at the Las Vegas wedding chapels on the Strip and in several of the casinos. Add extras, such as a rented bridal gown, flowers, and a video of the ceremony, and you'll whoop up the price. But, even so, the cost will be nothing compared with a reception at your local country club.

If you're pressed for time, there's A Little White Chapel at 1301 Las Vegas Boulevard S. where you can tie the knot for just $30 at the world's only Drive-Up Wedding Window. They offer twenty-four-hour service, and you don't even need to call ahead. There's also a 20-percent-off coupon available in the *Discover Nevada* bonus book.

The Sporting Life

It's possible that you can see more top sporting events in Las Vegas than anywhere else in the country. Not major league baseball or professional football, perhaps, but just about everything else. From professional world boxing titles and international table tennis championships to the National Finals Rodeo and top golf tournaments, Las Vegas is where a good deal of the country's sports action is.

Some of the events are free or low cost, such as the annual Las Vegas Invitational Slo-Pitch Senior Softball tournament, which takes place in August at various fields around the city; or the Las Vegas Holiday Prep Classic, in which high school basketball teams compete at UNLV North and South gyms just before Christmas.

Others, like championship boxing matches—held at Aladdin, Caesars Palace, MGM Grand, and Mirage—are definitely for the big spenders. But although ringside seats can cost hundreds of dollars—more if you buy the tickets from scalpers—you can see the boxers work out with their sparring partners prior to the big event for free. The more important the match, the earlier the boxers come into town. That means that workouts open to the public are usually the weekend before the fight for the biggest-name boxers, and in the first part of the week before the fight for lesser-knowns.

Games played at Cashman Field (850 Las Vegas Boulevard N., 702-386-7184; bus 113 or 208) by the Las Vegas Stars, a Triple A affiliate of the San Diego Padres, cost a lot less than major league games (a family of four can attend for about $20), and it's usually pretty good baseball. In fact, more than 110 former Stars players have made it to the majors, and the team is only celebrating its twelfth year in 1994. For information on whom the Stars are playing and when, call their hot line at 702-739-3900.

The Las Vegas Thunder Bolts of the International Hockey League brought professional hockey to Las Vegas with their

1993–94 inaugural season. With a home schedule of thirty-nine games, played at Thomas & Mack Stadium (4505 Maryland Parkway, 702-798-7825; bus 109, 201, or 302), ticket prices go from $9 to $15 for the top-price box seats. At the Las Vegas Speedway International (6000 Las Vegas Boulevard N., 702-643-3333) you can watch NASCAR stock-car races and NHRA-sanctioned drag racing (prices vary). Throughout the year, prestigious golf tournaments and tennis matches also take place at various Las Vegas venues.

Courts and Courses

But maybe you would rather play sports than watch someone else. If your idea of a great vacation involves swinging a tennis racquet, a golf club, or a marathon of racquetball games, you'll want to know what your choices of courts and courses are. The following will give you an idea of facilities that are open to the public and their fees.

Golf Courses

Facility, Address, Phone	Fees	
Angel Park, 100 S. Rampart (702-254-4653)	greens fee (with cart) club rental	$95 25
Black Mountain Golf and Country Club, 500 Greenway Rd. (702-565-7933)	greens fee (with cart) ($45 weekends, holidays)	40
Craig Ranch Golf Course, 628 Craig Rd. (702-642-9700)	greens fee cart club rental	14 7 8
Desert Rose, 5483 Club House Dr. (702-431-4653)	greens fee (with cart) ($39 weekends) club rental	60 15

Facility, Address, Phone	Fees	
Las Vegas Municipal, Decatur and Washington (702-646-3003)	greens fee club rental	21.95 18
The Legacy, 130 Par Excellence Dr. (702-897-2187)	greens fee (with cart)	$110–120
Los Prados Country Club, 5150 Los Prados Circle (702-645-5696)	greens fee Saturday, Sunday, holidays twilight rate club rental	30 40 25 20
The Mirage Golf Club, 3650 Las Vegas Blvd. (702-369-7111)	greens fee (with cart) twilight fee (after 2 P.M.) club rental	125 75 25
Painted Desert Country Club, 555 Painted Mirage Way (702-645-2568)	greens fee (with cart) club rental	95–100 25–40
Wildhorse Golf Club, 1 Showboat Club Dr. (702-434-9009)	greens fee (with cart) club rental	110–125 25–40
Las Vegas Hilton Country Club, 1911 E. Desert Inn Rd. (702-796-0013)	greens fee (with cart) Friday–Sunday	125 145
Sheraton Desert Inn Golf Course, Sheraton Desert Inn Hotel, Strip (702-733-4299)	greens fee/guests nonguests club rental	75 150 25
Sun City Summerlin Golf Club, 9201 Del Webb Blvd. (702-363-4373)	greens fee (with cart) club rental	95 20

By doing some comparison looking, you can see that green fees and club rentals do vary a lot. What you can't tell from prices alone is what the courses are like. Angel Park, for example, is unique in that it re-creates twelve of the most famous par-3 holes in the world, including the double green at St. Andrews and the Postage Stamp at Royal Troon. The best way to determine if a particular golf course is your kind of bargain is to eyeball it and read up on its specs, then equate cost with what you expect to get from the experience.

Tennis Courts

Facility, Phone	Number	Fees	
Aladdin Hotel (702-736-0330)	3 lighted	hotel guests nonguests 5 (per hour) daily racquet rental	$5 8
Alexis Park Hotel (702-796-3300)	2 lighted	court per hour (guests) racquet rental	5 5
Bally's Las Vegas Hotel (702-739-4598)	10, 5 lighted	guests per hour nonguests racquet rental	10 15 5
Caesars Palace Hotel (702-731-7786)	4 lighted	hotel guests nonguests	15 25
Frontier Hotel (702-734-0110)	2 lighted	hotel guests only	
Jackie Gaughan's Plaza Hotel (702-386-2110)	4 lighted	hotel guests only	
Las Vegas Hilton Hotel (702-732-5111)	6, 4 lighted	hotel guests only racquet rental	 10
Riviera Hotel (702-734-5110)	2 lighted	hotel guests free nonguests per hour	 $10
Sheraton Desert Inn (702-733-4577)	10 lighted	hotel guests free nonguests daily pass racquet rental	 10 10

| The Sporting House, 3205 Industrial Rd. (702-733-8999) | 2 | daily pass (can also be used for all club facilities) | 15 |
| Sunset Park, Sunset and Eastern (702-455-8200) | 8 lighted | | 2 |

Courts maintained by recreation departments are almost always less expensive than privately run tennis operations. However, classes sponsored by the departments, plus popularity with local residents, keeps most courts so busy that you may have a long wait.

Racquetball

Facility, Address, Phone	Number	Court Fee	
Caesars Palace 3570 Las Vegas Boulevard S. (702-731-7786)	4	$10 per hour for 2 players	
Las Vegas Racquetball Club, 1071 E. Sahara Ave. (702-733-1919)	12	per court per hour	$6
The Sporting House, 3025 Industrial Rd. (702-733-8999)	21	daily pass	15

Bowling

Facility, Address, Phone	Number of Lanes	Fees	
Gold Coast, 4000 W. Flamingo (702-367-7111)	72	per game shoes	$1.85 1.25

Facility, Address, Phone	Number of Lanes	Fees	
Sam's Town Bowling Center, 5111 Boulder Highway (702-454-8022)	56	per game seniors/juniors shoes	1.60 1.20 1.35
Santa Fe, 4949 Rancho Dr. N., (702-658-4995)	60	per hour per lane (up to 6 people) shoes	8–12 1.50
Showboat Bowling Lanes, 2800 E. Fremont (702-385-9153)	106	per game seniors/juniors shoes	2.05 1.55 1.75
Sunset Lanes, 4565 E. Sunset, Green Valley (702-736-2695)	40	per game 12 and under shoes	1.50–1.95 1.25 1.50

If you want to play at Sam's Town on Friday or Sunday mornings anytime from nine A.M. to noon, you'll get savings: 55¢ per game per person on Fridays; $4.50 per hour per lane on Sundays. At Santa Fe, Friday is ladies' day and Monday is seniors' day, with lane charges $5 an hour (up to six people playing). Showboat Bowling Lanes charges .75 per game, with free shoes daily, from one to seven A.M.

And now the for the bungee-jumping info. You go to Las Vegas Bungee Masters at 810 Circus Circus Drive (702-385-4321), rise to the top of the 201-foot tower via an air-conditioned "bungee elevator," pay your $79 ($20 for subsequent jumps on same day), take a look at the Strip below, and eeeeeeooooooooooouuuuuuuuu. If you think it's *expensive*, you *do* get a video of your jump and a membership card.

After-Dark Entertainment

Burning the candle at both ends is what Las Vegas is all about. You can't stop just because the sun goes down. In fact, for a lot of Las Vegas visitors, that's when the fun begins.

Although there are entertainment pundits who predict that the era of the megastar entertainer is on its way back in Las Vegas, right now the emphasis—as it has been in recent years—is on the big production show. Following are the major shows, where they are, and what they cost:

Show/Entertainer	Hotel/Casino		Price
Boylesque	Debbie Reynolds Hollywood Hotel/Casino		$24.95
Spellbound	Harrah's		29.95
Starlight Express	Las Vegas Hilton		19.50–45
Legends in Concert	Imperial Palace		29.50
Catch a Rising Star	Bally's		12.50
Hypnomania	Sahara		29.95
Country Tonite	Aladdin		17.95
	18 and under		11.95
Jubilee	Bally's		42.00
Copacabana	Rio	dinner	34.95
Splash	Riviera		39.50–49.50
La Cage	Riviera		18.95
Crazy Girls	Riviera		16.95
Comedy Club	Riviera		14.95
Comedy Stop	Tropicana		12.95
Folies-Bergère	Tropicana	cocktail	23.95
		dinner from	30.95
Arthur's Tournament	Excalibur	dinner	29.95
Viva Las Vegas	Sands	afternoon	10.00

Show/ Entertainer	Hotel/Casino		Price
Enter the Night	Stardust		24.90
City Lites	Flamingo	cocktail	20.95
		dinner from	28.50
Siegfried & Roy	Mirage		72.85
Cirque du Soleil	Treasure Island	adults	46.20
(Cirque de Soleil prices include tax)		under 12	23.10

Bally's Las Vegas Celebrity Room, Caesars Palace Circus Maximus, Desert Inns' Starlight Theatre, MGM Grand Hollywood Theatre, and, on occasion, Mirage, showcase big-name entertainers, with ticket prices ranging all the way to $1,000 in the case of Barbra Streisand's New Year's performances at the MGM Grand. The average admission to a headliner show is somewhere around $50. If the ticket price you're quoted doesn't include tax and tip, be sure to add in the enormous 17 percent tax (10 percent entertainment tax plus 7 percent state tax) as well as a 10 to 15 percent gratuity.

It's a rare production show that you can't get a discount on (usually $3 but sometimes $5) or that isn't included in its hotel's packages (one of the exceptions is Siegfried & Roy). Not all seats at the shows are created equal, so look at a seating chart before you buy your tickets. Tip: the seats where you'll have the most fun at the Las Vegas Hilton's Starlight Express, where tickets go from $19.15 to $45, are those onstage in the cheering section—the cheapest seats in the house.

Of course, it you're a high roller, you'll have no problem getting comped to any of the shows. When you're not a big-time spender, it's a little more difficult getting into the shows' VIP lines. But it can be done, provided you're planning to do some gambling. However, don't gamble just because you want free show tickets. Your losses may well exceed the ticket prices.

Slot club points, which we talk about in chapter 11, can often be used for admission to production shows. However, your best shot at free show tickets is by playing 21 or craps.

If there are two of you, assign the person who knows the game best as your designated player. Move from table to table at first, sizing up the action, playing a hand here and there. The pit boss, whose business it is to know what's going on, will have taken note of the fact that you're playing when you approach him later on.

After about an hour, go over to the pit boss and ask very pleasantly about the possibility of being comped to the cocktail show, reminding him in the course of the conversation that you've been at the tables for a while—this is a massageable point since the pit boss will only have a sense of the length of time you've been in the area. He will probably tell you to check back with him when you're done playing.

Stretch your legs, seek out another table that looks promising (the dealer seems friendly or on a run of bad luck), sip a free beverage, play a few hands, and report back to the pit boss when you're ready to leave. Be as creative as you want using this general approach, and chances are you'll get your free tickets.

I know one young man who is especially successful at getting comped. He wears the best casual clothes in his wardrobe, right down to the hand-stitched Italian shoes—guys in tank tops seldom get comped. His game is craps, and he always makes it a point to learn the stick and point men's names before he starts playing. "Hey, Larry (or Al or Pete)," he says, as he finds a place at the table timed to coincide with the pit boss's being close by, "haven't seen you in a while. How's it going?"

By the time he's ready to approach the pit boss, he has learned his or her name, too, and is able to use the knowledge to his advantage. In a relatively short time he's become a "regular," which works because (1) he's doing all the right things, and (2) casino personnel may know what's going on around them, but they can't remember all the people who've played in their casino two weeks before, let alone two months.

Sometime in the course of his table play and conversations with the pit boss, he lets them know his name, too—comp insurance for his future visits.

Though entertainment in the showrooms can cost big money, you don't have to spend a dime to watch many of the lounge shows and casino stage acts. Not that all the entertainment is first-rate. But if you don't like the show, just walk on to the next casino. Sooner or later you'll catch a group or two on their way to the top.

There's no cover and no minimum drink charge in most lounges, so you can get by by nursing a beer or soft drink. However, since lounge drink prices are usually higher than at the casino's regular bars, you can often see the show for less by sitting at a bar that's adjacent to the lounge. At the Sahara, for example, there's a great view of the lounge stage from the seats on the right side of the Casbar.

If you would like a free drink—alcoholic or soft—while you're in a casino, better have a few coins to put in the slot machines. Cocktail waitresses circulate regularly, but they only offer complimentary drinks to people who appear to be gambling.

In addition to evening performances in the casino showrooms, a few of the shows are also presented in the afternoon, and others are put on only at that time. An example of the latter is "Viva Las Vegas" in the Copa Room of the Sands, one of the longest-running afternoon shows on the Strip. The admission of $10 includes one drink, but two-admissions-for-the-price-of-one coupons are frequently in circulation.

Not So Make-believe Ballrooms

You'll find lots of places where you can give your dancing shoes a low-cost workout, both in the casinos and at nightspots throughout the city. Free Western dance lessons are given from 7:30 to 9 P.M. at the Western Dance Hall at Sam's Town (5111 Boulder Highway, 702-456-7777) Monday through Saturday.

After nine P.M., you can practice what you've learned to live music.

Free country dance lessons are offered at Rockabilly (3785 Boulder Highway, 702-641-5800), starting at seven-thirty nightly. Bus 107 goes out Boulder Highway.

And if you really love your country, you'll try to time your Las Vegas visit to the National Finals Rodeo in December, when country-dance parties are held at casinos and clubs all over town.

Area-51 (3665 S. Industrial, behind the Mirage 702-733-6366) features progressive dance music on Thursday, Friday and Saturday, starting at 10 P.M., while at Fremont Street Blues & Reggae Club (Fremont and 4th Streets; 702-594-4640), there's live music nightly.

There's live jazz and blues at Play It Again Sam (4120 Spring Mountain Road, 702-876-1550); and Hobnob (3340 S. Highland, 702-734-2426) is where local musicians like to hang out.

If You would rather spend your after-dark energy shooting hoops, Final Score Sports Bar at Sam's Town offers a basketball key court, electronic darts, pool tables, computerized golf and a sand volley ball court.

You can also dig live music outdoors on summer nights, when free bluegrass and country concerts are presented at Jaycee Park in August (St. Louis and Eastern, 702-386-6297; bus 204), and free jazz performances take place at Paradise Park (4470 Harrison Drive) on Saturdays in June. Incidentally, Jaycee Park also has a great walking track, so you might want to arrive early and get some exercise before the music begins.

One of the best places to find out what's happening as far as entertainment is concerned is in the Friday and Saturday editions of the *Las Vegas Review-Journal*. You'll find discount coupons there, too, such as the two-for-one in recent issues for King Arthur's Tournament at Excalibur.

Promises, Promises

Prostitution is legal in Nevada, but not in Clark County. That means Las Vegas. So be forewarned. However, there is naked mud-wrestling and there are all sorts of girlie shows in storefront clubs downtown and elsewhere in the city.

You'll also see ranks of freestanding newspaper dispensers along the Strip containing sex-for-sale advertisements, and ads for "escort services" in the yellow pages of the phone book. Let the buyer beware. In some cases, what's paid for is not delivered. In others it has been—sometimes, with fatal consequences.

Checking Out the Culture

Las Vegas is a university town, with a large segment of the population interested in cultural events—many production-show performers were classically trained. As a result, almost every evening there's a cultural event going on somewhere in the city.

It may be a concert at Artemus W. Ham Hall (4505 S. Maryland Parkway, 702-895-3801; bus 109, 201, or 302), where the Nevada Opera Theatre presents performances of such classics as *Madame Butterfly*. The Nevada Symphony also performs there. Many of the symphony's musicians earn their livings by playing six nights a week in the orchestras of the big production shows.

Most of the presentations at Ham Hall—and they have included performances by such groups as the Red Army Orchestra and Dance Ensemble, Prague Chamber Orchestra, Constanza Orchestra of Romania, and the St. Paul Chamber Orchestra—cost much less than you might imagine. That's because they're underwritten by such groups as the Nevada State Council on the Arts and the Musicians' Union and Music Performance Trust Fund. A concert by the Stuttgart Chamber Choir was among recent free performances.

Another popular venue for the arts is the UNLV Performing Arts Center on the University of Nevada Las Vegas campus (702-895-3801) where the Nevada Dance Theatre, the only professional ballet company in Nevada, performs. The dance troupe utilizes the services of world-renowned choreographers, and their performances are top-drawer. Opus Dance Ensemble of Las Vegas, founded in the early 1980s, is a nonprofit group composed of professional dancers and choreographers from shows on the Strip (702-732-9646).

The Nevada Humanities Committee sponsors events showcasing music, poetry, storytelling, dance, and other art forms at various halls and theaters, and it is responsible for bringing live performances to schoolchildren around the state.

Three groups—Las Vegas Little Theatre (702-383-0021), Actor's Repertory (702-438-7347), and New West Stage Company (702-876-NWSC) provide drama, comedy, and Broadway musicals for the theatergoing public. Among their 1996 productions were *Man of La Mancha* and *Someone to Watch Over Me*. Prices vary with the group and the production, but are mostly in the $8-to-$12.50 range, with discounts for students and seniors.

Whether it's a concert featuring Las Vegas' most popular gospel groups or a free performance of Verdi's Requiem, you'll find out what cultural events are going on while you're in Las Vegas by phoning the UNLV Performing Arts Center (702-895-3801), and checking the newspaper's entertainment pages.

6

Shopping/Souvenirs

Some people, as the bumper sticker says, were born to shop. They're happy anywhere as long as there's something to buy. Others would rather have minor surgery than spend two hours at a shopping mall.

Most of us fall somewhere in between. Shopping's fun when we can find lots of bargains. We savor trying to buy the Neiman-Marcus look at discount-store prices. It's great sport, too, when some of the stores are a bit different or funky or downright weird. In short, we like the kind of shopping you can find in Las Vegas.

Because of the city's tremendous tourist count, the number of commercial establishments is way out of proportion with the population. There are upscale shopping arcades in the major hotels, sleazy souvenir shops on the Strip between casinos. Megamalls. Factory outlets. An antiques mall. Neighborhood shopping centers. You can buy everything from religious tracts to feelthy postcards; designer grunge to thrift-shop chic; original Chagall paintings to desert scenes acrylicked on pink satin pillows with lots of gold fringe.

Las Vegas stores generally open at 9:30 or 10 A.M. and remain open until 5:30 or 6 P.M. Most mall stores open at 10 A.M. and close at 9 P.M., except on Saturday and Sunday nights when they're open until 6 P.M. And good news for night owls with money—some of the Forum Shops stay open until 11 P.M.

Just Looking Thanks

Shopping can be your activity of choice even if you don't plan to buy a thing. It can be entertaining, and at times educational, to look at art objects and the like that we have no intention of ever owning. And, too, in Las Vegas there are lots of baubles, bangles, and the like for sale that are fun to look at even though they're well out of most of our price ranges.

Multitudes of big spenders, you see, pass through Las Vegas on a daily basis, and a lot of wealthy people live in the city. Then there are the big winners who after hitting an $800 or $8,000 or $800,000 jackpot want to go out and spend that money. As a result, high-ticket items are the order of business in many of the casino arcade boutiques as well as at Fashion Show Mall and the Forum Shops on the Strip.

Largest of the hotel shopping arcades is Bally's, with forty stores showcasing everything from gourmet ice cream to haute couture. Caesars Palace Appian Way features some of Las Vegas' most exclusive shops along an elegant promenade, and resort wear is a specialty at Mirage's Esplanade. The Flamingo Hilton, Riviera, and Stardust are among the other hotels with tony arcade shops.

Fashion Show Mall, on the Strip between the Mirage and Frontier hotels, is about as upscale as a shopping mall can get. Anchored by Bullock's, Dillard's, Robinson-May, Neiman-Marcus, and Saks Fifth Avenue, its 145 stores include Sharper Image, Banana Republic, Benetton, and a clutch of galleries and jewelry stores.

Don't expect run-of-the-mall stores or surroundings at the Forum Shops either. For one thing, the statues talk. For another, the clouds and light of the domed ceiling provide a constantly changing sky overhead, so that in the morning you can behold the sun, and at night, the stars. The entrance to this Roman streetscape lined with such luxury shops as Gucci, Escada, Gianni Versace, and Louis Vuitton is in Caesars Palace, and it is worth the trek—even for confirmed nonshoppers. At the Festival Fountain, Bacchus and his entourage present a sound, light, and laser show daily, every hour beginning at ten A.M. If shopping at Saks Fifth Avenue, Neiman-Marcus and the Forum Shops ordinarily seems out of the economic question, consider catching one of their sales. According to women who have worked at Saks for several years, the store's best sale is from December 26 through the first of the next year. Furs are an especially good buy, and selected ready-to-wear is marked down drastically.

Those in the know at Neiman-Marcus advise that though they have both summer and winter "last call" sales, when all sale merchandise is marked down still further, the sale that begins in mid-January is definitely the best. Savings, they say, can be as much as 60 percent.

Browsing the Galleries

At Gallery of History (Fashion Show Mall; 10 A.M.–6 P.M., Monday–Wednesday and Saturday; 10 A.M.–9 P.M., Thursday and Friday; noon–5 P.M., Sunday; 702-731-2300), there are letters written by George Washington and other famous people, autographed photographs, and other valuable documents. The most expensive item in the collection is a six-page letter by Albert Einstein about his theory of relativity. The letter is priced at $1,250,000, but it won't cost you a dime to take a look.

Also in Fashion Show Mall, Centaur Galleries (702-737-0004) handles fine art such as watercolors by Leroy Neiman and signed prints by Marc Chagall. Hours are the same as those of the Gallery of History.

Debora Spinover Fine Art (1775 E. Tropicana Avenue in the Liberace Plaza, 702-739-0072) specializes in original limited editions and animation art by such internationally acclaimed artists as Andy Warhol and Peter Max. Originals by Warhol, which might bring $7,000 to $8,000, are considered bargains now compared to the prices they commanded in the eighties.

Buying art works, however, doesn't necessarily have to cost

a lot of money. Especially when you shop for works by artists who live in the area and haven't established national or international reputations.

To see works focusing on Nevada and Southwest themes by two hundred local artists, go to Las Vegas Artists Cooperative, 4300 Meadows Lane (10 A.M.–9 P.M. Monday-Friday; 10 A.M.–6 P.M., Saturday and Sunday; 702-887-0761). Trinity Black Art Gallery & Custom Framing (2657 Las Vegas Boulevard N.; 702-399-1125) handles the works of African-American artists.

Mall Cruising

The Boulevard Mall, which completed a $60-million expansion in 1992, is located five minutes east of the Strip on Maryland Parkway between Desert Inn Road and Twain (buses 109, 112, and 203). Boulevard Mall's four anchors are JC Penney, Dillard's, Broadway Southwest, and Sears. Sesame Street General Store, Nature Company, and Bombay Company are among the more interesting of the 123 stores in the complex.

The Meadows Mall, two miles west of downtown at the intersection of U.S. 95 and Valley View (buses 103, 104, 207, and 208) has department stores from the same chains as Boulevard and is twenty or so stores larger. The mall provides its own trolley that transports shoppers from the Downtown Transportation Center (DTC) to the mall in less than eight minutes.

The Spanish-style Factory Stores (five miles south of Tropicana Avenue on Las Vegas Boulevard S., bus 301 or 302, transfer at Vacation Village to 108) is composed of fifty name-brand outlets that offer savings of 20 to 70 percent off the items' retail prices. This discount mall is a particularly good place to shop for shoes at cut-rate prices, with Nine West, Florsheim, and Converse among the half dozen stores specializing in footwear. You'll also find some good buys on luggage and housewares. An especially good time to shop the outlet stores is in January, when the discounted merchandise is marked down even further.

The newest discount mall, Belz Factory Outlet World, not far from the Factory Stores on Las Vegas Boulevard S., is fully enclosed, climate-controlled, and presents a state-of-the-art laser show every hour on the domed ceiling in front of the food court. It's also the only nonsmoking shopping facility in Nevada. Besides all that, of course, there are stores—seventy-two of them, where savings of up to 75 percent are advertised.

Belz Factory Outlet World is a great place to shop for children's clothes, with Buster Brown, Bugle Boy, OshKosh B'Gosh and Nike among others that youngsters favor.

Looking for Something a Bit Different?

Holy Cow!, which we've mentioned a couple of times already in this book, has a gift shop with nothing but "cowllectibles" for sale. Black-and-white holstein-patterned napkins, coasters, bib shorts, boxer shorts, coffee mugs, and cream pitchers, plus an array of a hundred other bovine-themed items, are fun to look at even if they don't fit into your decorating schemes. And check out the Christmas tree ornaments. The cows in lace dresses are especially charming.

Cat's Meow (2234 Paradise Road, 702-734-7337), as you may have guessed, is devoted to felines—real and collectible, as well as cat toys and equipment. Precious, Smokey, Ebony, and Duffy roam the aisles and sometimes sit on the display tables. From cookie jars to hand-painted ties to afghans and gift wrap, everything in the store has a cat/kitten motif. "Jingle Cats" (the tape is $10; the CD, $16) features cats singing Christmas carols, and there are cat greeting cards, too. Gifts for cats include a pup tent (shouldn't it be called a kitty tent?) that's described as "purrfect for hiding their treasures in," and a place mat picturing shrimp and sardines that's designed to keep kitty's dish from slipping.

Shepler's (3035 E. Tropicana Avenue, 702-898-3000; and 4700 W. Sahara at Decatur, 702-258-2000) advertise themselves as the "world's largest Western stores." We don't know whether they are or not, but we do know they carry a huge selection of Western wear—boots, belt buckles, bolo ties, and all. And speaking of boots, if you want to buy some at a bargain, Shepler's holds a Thanksgiving Week Boot Blowout, with certain models marked down substantially. Their advertisement, found in tourist brochure racks, is good for an extra 10 percent off regular and sale merchandise.

For more bargains on Western wear, the year-end tent sale at Sam's Town features discounted items from the hotel/casino's Western Emporium shops. The sale begins in late November and lasts a month.

Ray's Beaver Bag (727 Las Vegas Boulevard S., 702-386-8746) specializes, it would seem, in outfitting pioneers and mountain men. There are racks of gingham dresses and sunbonnets, coonskin caps, leather pouches and bags, and, of course, handmade moccasins. Frontier supplies include hunting knives and tomahawks, cast-iron skillets, and snake-tanning kits, plus lots more. It's better than a good surplus store for browsing around.

Whether you're the reincarnation of one of Macbeth's witches or just an ordinary tourist, you'll enjoy Bell, Book, and Candle (1725 E. Charleston Road, 702-384-6807), a stock-up station for potions, talismans, crystal balls, magic charms, and other witchcraft supplies. Classes are also conducted.

If you're in the market for cans of Mace, stun guns, or bulletproof vests, you'll find them at the Spy Factory (2228 Paradise Road, 702-893-0779). The place is a wanna-be espionage agent's delight with wiretap and bugging devices, electronic surveillance equipment, and rearview sunglasses. And hey! There is even a video camera you could disguise as a pack of cigarettes.

Rebelbilia (4700 Maryland Parkway, 702-739-9200) is the official UNLV team shop, carrying a large selection of red-and-gray Runnin' Rebel merchandise including the usual pennants, sweatshirts, caps, and mugs with the school logo. But there are also items like barbecue grills, trash cans, and little lights that you hook up to car headlights.

Car back home missing a hubcap? Then go to Hub Cap Annie's (1602 E. Charleston Boulevard, 702-387-1148), which claims to be the largest collection in the world.

And what about something to bring back to the kids? Most people don't think of museum shops as places to find gifts for children. But while the prices may not always be cheap, quality is consistently high. At the Lied Museum there are microscopes, children's musical instruments, and building materials such as magnetic blocks. And don't miss the Read-a-Mat place mats. One shows the various ballet positions, another is a map of the United States, and still another teaches the Spanish alphabet.

At the Museum of Natural History gift shop, little rubber snakes, dinosaurs, and sea creatures as well as Educational Insights games are among the items for sale in the three rooms.

Ethnic Shopping Stops

Although it looks like any other neighborhood shopping plaza, the stores at the Commercial Center (953 E. Sahara Avenue) are predominantly Asian. More than a half dozen Asian restaurants—with new ones opening each year—are part of the complex.

Oriental Foods (702-735-2778) and Asian Market (702-734-7653) are fascinating to browse, even if you don't buy the dried seaweed and preserved cats' tongues. If you like to cook Asian dishes, you will be happy to find fish paste, lemongrass, *hoisin* sauce, and other ingredients that aren't readily available in most supermarkets. The stores also carry rice steamers, woks, cookbooks, and inexpensive porcelain dishes for serving oriental food.

At David Ming Oriental Art Goods (702-737-0277), hand-painted screens and silk kimonos are the stars, along with a quality selection of bamboo and rattan furniture.

Afrocentric Center's (705 W. Van Buren Street, 702-647-2242) focus is on everything about or for African Americans, from books and tapes to fabric and ready-made clothing, that they can find to sell.

Bookstore Browsing

People with the notion that Las Vegas is all fun and games may be surprised to learn that, in addition to the mainstream bookstores, there are about twenty-four other booksellers in town. They may be rare-book dealers, paperback exchanges, or stores that specialize in certain kinds of publications.

Two of several businesses that specialize in rare and out-of-print books are Albion Book Company (2466-G E. Desert Inn Road, 702-792-9554) and Americana Collectibles (3020 W. Charleston Boulevard, 702-597-2911).

Native Son Books at the Afrocentric Center (1301 D Street, 702-647-0101) handles new and used books, tapes, videos, and posters about the Afro-American experience.

Page after Page (1456 E. Charleston Boulevard, 702-384-1690) specializes in domestic and foreign comics, movie magazines, role-playing games, and Japanese animation as well as Disney products. Bob Coffin Books (3661 S. Maryland Parkway, 702-733-9378) stocks Nevada books and maps, USGS surveys, and material on geology, mining, and the Southwest.

Another out-of-the-ordinary bookhandler is Psychic Eye Book Shop (953 E. Sahara Avenue, 702-369-6622), where you can buy books on the occult and astrology. The shop also carries herbs, crystals, and amulets.

And, if you really must know, the adult bookstores are primarily on lower Fremont Street, Flamingo and Paradise roads.

Two good places to shop for record albums from the past are the Music Room (1406 Las Vegas Boulevard S., 702-387-3366) and Record City (553 E. Sahara, 702-369-6446). The former specializes in recordings by the likes of Fats Waller, the Dorsey

Brothers, Benny Goodman, and other jazz/swing greats, while the latter carries rare rock from the fifties through the seventies as well as some wonderful Broadway musicals and movie sound tracks.

Shopping Alternative

People who live in Las Vegas dress up for special occasions held in the evenings. I mean *really* dress up. Tuxedos for the men. For the women, long gowns with slit skirts and lots of spangles; beaded numbers that cost a fortune if you buy them retail. If, after you arrive, you're invited to a Las Vegas charity ball or gala and haven't a thing to wear, you may want to rent some fancy duds. A wide choice of gowns, dresses, and cocktail suits—including originals by top designers—can be rented at Designer Rentals for Her (4559 W. Flamingo, 702-364-4696), Renta-Dress (2240 Paradise, 702-796-6444), and A Bridal & Prom (located in the Hacienda Hotel, 702-597-5915). Prices range from $55 for an ordinary cocktail dress to $700 for a beaded designer gown.

More than three dozen businesses rent men's formal wear. Tux rental prices—including shoes and accessories—start at about $45. There's a substantial difference in what is charged, so it will pay to compare prices.

If it's a bad-hair day, you might want to go to Serge's Showgirl Wigs (900 Karen Avenue, 702-732-1015), the country's largest wig and hairpiece retailer where ten thousand wigs, toupees, and other hairpieces are priced at $60 and up. Serge's ads say "Where the Stars and Showgirls Buy Their Wigs" and include a $10-off-any-wig offer to shoppers who present the ad at the time of purchase.

Alternative Shopping

You won't be in Las Vegas long before you notice the pawnshops in Glitter Gulch and along the Strip. Much of their merchandise comes from gamblers who hock their watches or boom boxes or blowtorches for a little more gambling money and never redeem the pledged items. But pawnshops get their merchandise from other sources, too.

They may buy remaining stock from retail stores going out of business, or from fire sales. Other items come from stores that take used goods, such as cameras and stereo equipment, on trade. And yes, it's possible that stolen goods pass over some of their counters, though the police department's pawnshop detail works hard to prevent this from happening.

Even if you don't plan on buying anything, Las Vegas pawnshops are intriguing to browse around. The array of items can be pretty incredible—everything from guitars hanging from the ceilings and trays of flashy diamond rings to turquoise belt buckles and pneumatic drills.

If you do plan to make any pawnshop purchases, it's essential to know the going prices for items you want to buy. For example, a recent pawnshop sortie found that an identical model single-lens reflex camera was marked at various prices from $100 to $265, and the price for the same model in the used equipment of a local camera store was $175.

Among the pawnshops that are fun to look around, Ace Loan Company (212 N. 3rd Street), Pioneer Pawn Shop, (111 N. First; established 1935), and Stoney's (126 S. First) are the old-timers. You can even hock your car if you need to—or buy one at any of several auto pawn operations. If you want to make a purchase at any pawnshop, don't accept the first price you're quoted. Maybe not the second or third either.

Las Vegas has so many antique shops that the dyed-in-the-past collector could well spend an entire vacation poking about their nooks and crannies.

Antique Square (2014–2026 E. Charleston Boulevard) makes the job a little easier logistically. A dozen different shops make up the complex, and while Nicholas & Osvaldo (702-386-0238) is perhaps the most impressive of the group, you'll want to look at the costume jewelry at Gagliano's Antiques (702-366-8561). The handmade quilts and embroidered linens at Granny's Nook (702-598-1983) are special. At all these shops, look under counters and dig through boxes to find treasures other shoppers may have missed, and be sure to bargain. Devere's Curiosity Shop (702-366-8555) is a treasure trove sort of place, where you have to dig through boxes of stuff but are likely to come up with some interesting finds.

About a dozen other antiques and collectibles shops are concentrated in the same area on E. Charleston Boulevard, approximately two miles from downtown.

Silver Horse Antiques (702-385-2700) has items from the past in all shapes and sizes, categories, and conditions. Part of the eclectic inventory is a one-chair barbershop, complete with the traditional straight-edge razors, hair clippers, and tonic in a case on the wall. Don't go into the Silver Horse's back room on the hour—or do, if you want to hear lots of clocks chiming and tolling at the Sunshine Clock Shop.

For fashions from decades past, try Déjà Vu (2046 E. Charleston Boulevard, 702-382-1165). Remember that the closer a shop is to the Strip, the higher its prices will usually be.

To my mind, Las Vegas' most intriguing antiques experiences are the antiques auctions (usually held twice yearly, in spring and fall) by Victorian Casino Antiques (1421 S. Main, 702-382-2466. Collectors come from around the country for these two-day events, which are a bargain if you collect antiques and plan to get in on the bidding, since it costs first-time customers $100 to register. If you're a successful bidder, the money is applied to your purchase. If not, you'll have spent your $100 for all the free food and drink you can hold.

Additional Alternatives

Thrift shops aren't the sort of places most people think about when doing their vacation shopping, but they're ideal when you want to buy a "throwaway" item to use exclusively while you're in town—an umbrella when it decides to rain all day (and that can happen in Las Vegas), a pair of running shorts when you've forgotten yours at home and don't want to buy new ones.

Many of the thrift shops are strung out along Charleston Boulevard, among them the Junior League Repeat Boutique (300 E. Charleston Boulevard, 702-384-6941), and the St. Jude's Good Buy Thrift Shop (1717 E. Charleston Boulevard, 702-386-0772), which benefits the children at St. Jude's Ranch in nearby Boulder City.

The two biggest swap meets in town—in fact they're billed as "the biggest swap meets in Nevada"—are Fantastic Indoor Swap Meet (Decatur Boulevard at W. Oakey) and Gemco Indoor Swap Meet (Boulder Highway at E. Sahara), held on Friday, Saturday, and Sunday of each week. Merchandise varies from one weekend to the next, with more than one hundred vendors taking part in the giant cut-rate shopping expos.

Mountains of notepads, bolts of ribbon and lace, pseudo-sheepskin seat covers, old baseball cards, hundreds of bottles of nail-polish remover—you may find real bargains if the day's items for sale dovetail with what you're hoping to buy. Admission to each of the swap meets is $1 for adults. Kids twelve and under get in free. There are widely circulated two-for-one admission coupons, good at either of the locations, and 50¢-off coupons also appear frequently in Las Vegas newspapers.

You might not think of shopping at pawnshops, antiques stores, thrift shops, and flea markets when you're on other vacations, but in Las Vegas—due to the nature of the city—there's generally a different selection of merchandise than you'd find in other parts of the country. Can you imagine coming upon porno pamphlets from the forties in Topeka? And besides pawnshops and the like are all places where we can haggle, which makes finding real bargains an intriguing possibility.

Getting a Good Deal

While you're looking for discounts on meals, attractions, and gambling, keep your eye peeled for store discount coupons. They will often be for sizable amounts, like the coupon that

offers $5 off a purchase of $30 or more at Herbs & Spice (4750
W. Sahara at Decatur, 702-878-4042), where they carry Crabtree
& Evelyn products as well as a wide selection of spices, herbs,
and books.

Ethel M. Chocolates, which are about as expensive (and
delicious) as any candy you can buy in Nevada, soften the price
blow with a variety of add-ons throughout the year—from a free
double-decker pecan pattie when you buy one pound, to one
free pound of chocolates when you buy two or three pounds.
Incidentally, the individual chocolates cost about 50¢ each.

You'll find coupon discounts on specified items, too, such
as 30 percent off the retail price of a canvas travel bag at the
Marshall Rousso store in the Sands Hotel. These are great only if
you really want to buy the specific article.

Coupons that prove especially valuable are those that offer a
discount at any one of a number of stores, such as a 10 percent
coupon in the Sampler Shoppe's brochure that is good at any of
the businesses in this antiques and interior-design mall.

Among Your Souvenirs

My vote for "no-cost Las Vegas souvenir" goes to the photo
postcards at Binion's Horseshoe, downtown. You can have your
picture taken in front of a million dollars in cash at absolutely
no charge.

Other photographic mementos that would undoubtedly
become keepsakes are the pictures taken at the photo concession on the lower level of Excalibur. For $30, you can have a
five-by-seven-inch picture taken of one or two people, dressed in
a choice of medieval costumes. With three or four people in the
group, it costs $40; for five or six, $50. Additional photos are $10
each. Upstairs at the magazine concession on the second floor,
you can have your photo on the cover of a magazine for $19.95
or on a T-shirt for $24.95.

When you want souvenirs that truly exemplify Las Vegas, go
to the Gambler's General Store (800 S. Main Street,

702-382-9903). It's a big establishment, with lots of floor space devoted to gambling paraphernalia such as pool, poker, and craps tables; genuine antique slot machines and reproductions of them; watches with slot machines and playing cards on their faces (kings on the men's watches, queens on the women's).

There are bins of poker chips, hundreds of decks of cards, thousands of dice. Racks hold some twelve-hundred different gambling-related books, and if you're looking for clothes—how about a necktie with a royal flush on it?

For personalized chips and casino supplies, you can go to Paul-Son Dice & Cards (2121 S. Industrial, 702-384-2525).

The mother of souvenir stands is the Bonanza Gift & Souvenir Shop (just south of Vegas World), billed as the largest souvenir store in the world. In this case, quantity doesn't necessarily equate with quality—or taste. Which makes this the ideal place to go if you're in the market for something particularly tacky to bring home to friends, like the toilet seats embellished with gambling symbols or the sparkly Lucite clocks with dice marking the hours.

So look around. You'll find that in Las Vegas a bargain—like beauty—is in the eye of the beholder.

7

♠

Sightseeing

With all the neon attractions, you would forgive Las Vegas if it had nothing else. But, in reality, the natural beauty and wonders of the surrounding country by themselves make southern Nevada a worthwhile tourist destination. Especially for bargain hunters.

That's because the best glitz-free sightseeing can cost you no more than a tank of gas and/or a day's rental fee for a car. Sure, you *can* take a $179.50 flight over the Grand Canyon or a $39 dinner cruise on Lake Mead, but you'll find that the no- or low-costers are the real stars of the Las Vegas excursion picture.

We've limited our excursions to those that can be reached from Las Vegas in less than two hours. The reason is simple. Three or four hours away and you're at southern Utah's national parks or in the Los Angeles orbit—and that's territory to fill a dozen other guidebooks.

We've also confined our chosen destinations to those within Nevada, with the exceptions of Lakes Mead and Mojave, portions of whose shorelines lie in Arizona.

House Tour

You may want to start out by driving along the residential streets where you'll find some of the city's most spectacular homes. But don't they look just like ritzy houses in other parts of the country? you ask. Not quite. For, you see, the flamboyance of Las Vegas show biz has spilled over into its pricey residential areas as well. Spotlights, exotic plants, extravagant pools and pool houses, plus some rather unusual architectural themes will keep you rubbernecking. One of the best areas to cruise is that around Rancho Circle northwest of the Strip. Another is in the neighborhood around Sunset Park.

Candy and Cactus

Heading east on Tropicana Avenue, then following Mountain Vista to Sunset Way, you'll pass by the big fence-enclosed spreads like Wayne Newton's on your way to the Ethel M. Candy Factory.

At the factory, visitors file slowly past a long stretch of plate glass, looking at what is everyone's image of the perfect candy plant. Workers are dressed all in white, their hair covered with white baseball-style hats or hairnets. They toil at stainless-steel tables and mixing machines in a large, airy room with spotless white walls, making candies and wrapping them in jewel-colored foil.

When Forrest Mars sold his interest in the Mars Candy Company—makers of such favorites as Snickers, Milky Way, and M&M's—he agreed not to go into competition with the buyers.

Later, the story goes, he grew bored, so began producing a noncompeting type of candy—gourmet chocolates named for his mother, Ethel. There are more than fifty flavors, including several with liqueurs in their fillings.

The free tour of the immaculate plant is not only informative, you're rewarded with the complimentary candy of your choice at its end. Outside is a delightful 2.5-acre cactus garden, where you can spend a pleasant half hour adding to your knowledge of these desert succulents. The plants, which are clearly identified, include some rare species that you're unlikely to see elsewhere.

If you can avoid the temptation of buying a box or two of the chocolates at the candy shop, the experience will cost you absolutely nothing. The factory and gardens are open 8:30 A.M. to 7 P.M. (800-438-4356). You can also make this trip by bus, taking the Strip bus 301 to the Vacation Village, then transferring to bus 212.

For more factory tours and free samples, go on to Kidd's Marshmallow Factory (8203 Gibson Road, Henderson; 702-564-5400) where they make marshmallow novelties as well as the regular marshmallows. To get to Kidd's, where self-guided tours are from 9 A.M. to 4:30 P.M. daily, drive on U.S. 95 south from Las Vegas and take the Sunset Road exit. Turn left at the light, drive half a mile to Gibson Road. Turn right and drive another mile and a half to the copper-topped building.

At nearby Ocean Spray's Cranberry World West (1301 American Pacific Drive; 702-566-7160) visitors can look at harvesting exhibits and watch the bottling process. The gift shop carries dozens of cranberry-themed items—from cranberry glass and gumballs to relish and recipe books. Cranberry World West is open daily 9 A.M. to 5 P.M.

Headin' Out West

One of my favorite excursions is to Red Rock Canyon National Conservation Area, not much more than twenty minutes driving time from the Strip (drive west on Charleston Boulevard until you reach the well-marked turnoff). On the eastern slopes of the Spring Mountains, the Red Rock escarpment rises three thousand feet, the result of violent geologic shifting thousands of years ago. Green vegetation, including ponderosa pines, decorates cracks, crannies, and crevices. Mountain streams with mini-waterfalls splash and tumble during winter and spring. It's an area where nature lovers could easily spend every day of their Las Vegas stay. Stop first at Red Rock Vista, about a mile past the highway turnoff. There, you can view the striated formation in all its majesty. A bit farther along the thirteen-mile loop road, you'll come to the visitor center, where you can pick up a free map of the park and buy the topographical map, both of which are essential if you plan to do any major hiking. A recorded self-guided tour will give you an overview of the area, and the center's bookstore is stocked with a good selection of reading material about flora, fauna, geology, and the like.

If you want to hike, you'll have quite a choice, ranging from a strenuous fourteen-mile round-trip to the top of the escarpment to easy one- to two-mile jaunts. Among the most popular treks are the Moenkope Loop, an easy two-mile trail through cottontop barrel cactus, creosote plants, blackbrush, and yucca. The six-mile Lamadre Spring trip follows a trail to the spring, which provides the water supply for bighorn sheep and other wildlife. It's classed as moderately strenuous.

Ice Box Canyon is a 2.5-mile round-tripper, which is moderately difficult and involves some rock scrambling. This is a good choice for warmer days because, as its name implies, the canyon is cooler than surrounding areas.

If you spend your Red Rock time driving the loop, be sure to stop once in a while to enjoy the world around you. With the aid of binoculars, you may be able to spot bighorn sheep, gray fox, bobcats, and wild burros at the higher elevations. Even if you don't spy any of the larger animals, you're sure to see squirrels and a whole bird book full of orioles, tanagers, wrens, hummingbirds, and other species.

Back on Charleston Road (also called State Route 159 in this section), you can continue on to Spring Mountain Ranch State Park, a ranch formerly owned by Vera Krupp of the munitions family and later by Howard Hughes. Admission to the park, which includes picnic facilities, is $5 per car.

On summer evenings outdoor productions of such musical comedies as *My Fair Lady* and *Seven Brides for Seven Brothers* are presented under the stars on the Spring Mountain stage. Admission is $5 for adults, $3 for seniors, students, and the handicapped on Wednesday and Thursday nights; $7 and $4 on Friday and Saturday. Children under the age of six are admitted free. Bring a blanket or lawn chairs, a picnic supper, and sweaters. Phone 702-594-PLAY for information.

A bit farther along the road is Bonnie Springs/Old Nevada, described in more detail in chapter 10, "Family Fun."

Moving Up in the World

When summer temperatures sizzle in Las Vegas, people in the know head for Mt. Charleston, thirty-five miles northwest of Las Vegas off U.S. Highway 95 (take the Kyle Canyon turnoff). Granted, it's not as cool as an air-conditioned casino, but it's usually from twenty to thirty degrees cooler than it is outdoors, on the Strip.

Savvy Las Vegans head for Mt. Charleston, too, when winter snows hit the southern-Nevada high spots. For though you can't by any stretch say the skiing rivals Aspen or Alta, snowmaking equipment guarantees powder on the slopes, and there are good places for sledding and other snow play, too.

Ski facilities include three chairlifts, which take passengers to more than forty acres of maintained bunny, intermediate, and expert slopes. For cross-country skiers, Scout Canyon, Mack's Canyon, and Bristlecone Trail are great for touring.

Whether you explore the park by car, on skis, snowshoes, foot, or bicycle, you'll want to plan to eat outdoors, as Mt. Charleston is one of Nevada's all-time great picnic places. Cathedral Rock, Old Mill, Robber's Roost, and Deer Creek are among the areas where you'll find facilities for dining *alfresco*.

Seasoned backpackers will enjoy the challenge of climbing to the summit of Mt. Charleston (11,918 feet). One trail to the top begins in Lee's Canyon and is an eleven-mile hike round-trip. The trailhead for another (nine miles) is at Cathedral Rock. To avoid coming back in the dark, most hikers make at least one overnight camp. When you hike, be sure to stay on the marked trails, especially at the higher elevations.

Less experienced hikers can choose from a variety of trails, including one to the majestic Cathedral Rock and another to Deer Creek. One of the loveliest hikes in springtime is the four-hour trek to Mary Jane and Big Falls in upper Kyle Canyon. The ranger station, located in Kyle Canyon, is the place to obtain maps and information about the area (702-872-5486).

Driving is best with the windows down so that you can smell as well as look at the vegetation of the different climatic zones you pass through on your climb up. Joshua trees, yucca—and, in spring, desert wildflowers—carpet the valley floor. When you reach five thousand feet, you'll see piñion pine, juniper, sage, and rabbitbrush.

Another thousand feet higher and you'll be in mountain mahogany, ponderosa pine, and blueberry territory, with springtime blossoms of such species as penstemon. Although the paved road ends at seventy-five-hundred feet, you can look up to see the tortured branches of five-thousand-year-old bristlecone pine, believed by some botanists to be the oldest plant species existing today.

Permanent Mt. Charleston residents include several hundred people who commute each day to Las Vegas, and Palmer chipmunks, which are found nowhere else in the world. And though you most likely won't see them, coyotes, fox, bighorn sheep, elk, deer, bobcats, and cougar live there, too.

Exploring Mt. Charleston by bicycle can be expensive, unless you have your own bike. Downhill Bicycle Tours, Inc. (702-897-8287), offers "breakfast roll" and "lunch roll" tours, which include pickup at a central Strip location and transportation up the mountain. Participants ride the eighteen miles downhill, then are transported back to the Strip. The tour costs $65 per person, with one-half off if you bring your own bike. There's also a coupon that's readily available for $10 off on the purchase of two tours, which cuts the cost a tad.

A Different Jurassic Park

During the Jurassic period, Mother Nature started going wild making red sandstone formations out of great dunes of sand. Through the next hundred million years, wind and water carved a six-mile-long depression we now know as the Valley of Fire

State Park (admission $4 per vehicle). About fifty-five miles northeast of Las Vegas (take Route 15 north, turning off at State Route 169), the area is a fantasy of domes, pinnacles, and spires in colors ranging from crimson and scarlet to deep purple, brilliant orange, and the palest shades of pink.

At the visitor center—a good first stop before you begin your explorations—you'll find maps, trail guides, and books on the region's history, geology, and ecology. Exhibits explain the natural forces that came into play to create the park's geologic wonders. And don't miss the tortoise habitat, where you can get a close-up look at this endangered species.

The Valley has been inhabited off and on by humans for more than five thousand years—some sources say twenty-thousand—and the marks they have left upon it are among the park's most interesting features. Members of each succeeding group, from the Fremont culture to the Anasazi, the Yuma, and more recent Paiutes, left messages incised upon the rocks.

Some of these petroglyphs served as road maps, perhaps others as billboards or signs to attract the attention of subsequent travelers. There are religious symbols and figures from the everyday life of hundreds and thousands of years ago.

The best views of the petroglyphs are at Atlatl Rock and in Petroglyph Canyon. Many of the carvings on the rock depict an ancient spear-throwing stick called the atlatl in one of the Aztec dialects. They are believed to predate A.D. 500, when the bow and arrow replaced the *atlatl* in southern Nevada.

Petroglyph Canyon is a narrow passage north of the visitor center whose walls are decorated with rare kachina figures (they're tucked away in a spot above one's customary line of vision), bighorn sheep, dancers, and clan signs.

The park's most unusual formation is Elephant Rock, said to resemble the mammoths which roamed the earth many thousands of years ago. Beehive Rocks are symmetrically weathered boulders that look like giant hives. As you might imagine, the more inaccessible areas of the park have been popular with directors of film and TV westerns, since they don't have to contend with modern-day nuisances such as power lines and phone poles.

It only takes fifteen or twenty minutes to drive through the Valley, but you'll probably want to get out and stretch your legs. A variety of self-guided trails range from those that are less than a mile and easy to walk to longer ones that are a lot more difficult. One of the shorter self-guided trails leads to Mouse's Tank, a series of catch basins named for a turn-of-the-century Native American called Mouse, who was holed up there (a) hiding out from the law or (b) stayed there after he was banished from his tribe, depending on which version of the story you hear. Two other trails lead to 225-million-year-old petrified logs.

Throughout the park, the rock catchments (also called tanks or *tinajas*) that collect water when it rains are where you're most likely to spot the birds, reptiles, mammals, and insects that inhabit the Valley.

Awe inspiring as the Valley of Fire is, it's not a trip that you'll want to make in the dead of summer, when temperatures are sizzling.

Lost City Museum

Twelve miles north of Valley of Fire State Park in the little town of Overton, the Lost City Museum contains one of the most complete collections of early Pueblo Indian artifacts in the Southwest. Museum displays span the period of the desert culture of ten thousand years ago, when man hunted now-extinct species such as the mammoth and the ground sloth, to the Mormon farmers who first settled the Valley in 1865.

In addition to the exhibits, several Pueblo-style houses of wattle and daub have been reconstructed on their foundations, and plants used by the early Indians are part of the surrounding landscape.

About a half-hour drive northeast of Overton, Mesquite—on the Nevada-Utah border—is the one of the state's fastest growing gambling spots. About half an hour farther on I-15, St. George, Utah, is known for its summer Shakespeare performances.

An Awesome Bargain

About half an hour south of Las Vegas on U.S. Highway 93, Hoover Dam is considered one of the seven engineering wonders of the modem world. For eons, the Colorado River had periodically run amok as it raced on its way to the Gulf of California. After man began farming along the river, he often found his lands flooded and valuable topsoil eroded. In dry years, crops shriveled and cattle died.

Then, in 1931, construction began on the first arch-gravity-type dam ever built. Work continued virtually twenty-four hours a day until 1935, when the 726-foot-high dam was dedicated by President Franklin D. Roosevelt.

Since that time, some 29 million visitors have toured the massive facility, which annually produces enough electricity to provide a half million homes with power for one year. It also furnishes water to land downriver, in accordance with demand.

Guided tours of the dam—you actually go inside the structure—are offered from 9 A.M. to 4:15 P.M. daily. Admission is a real bargain at $5 for adults, $2.50 for people over sixty-five, and free for children under nine (702-293-8367). Even if you don't take the tour, you'll get a thrill just looking at the gigantic concrete structure from one of the viewpoints on either side of the river.

If you want to learn more about the dam and the people who built it, the Boulder City Hoover Dam Museum (444 Hotel Plaza, 702-294-1988) contains photographs, souvenirs, coins, stamps, and other artifacts as well as dressed mannequins and furnishings reflecting the actual conditions of the workers' lives.

While you're in Boulder City, you might want to drive around to look at the bungalows built in the 1930s, which give the town a charm unlike that of any other place in southern Nevada.

The Biggest Lake by a Dam Site

When the Colorado River was backed up by Hoover Dam, it formed the largest manmade body of water in the United States, with 550 miles of freshwater shoreline. Lake Mead's beauty is dramatic rather than pretty, with stark rock formations forming the backdrop for its aquamarine waters—more like a painting by Salvador Dalí than one by Winslow Homer.

If you've decided to rent a houseboat (see chapter 3, "Accommodations"), you'll be able to spend your time relaxing in a deck chair. Or maybe you'll throw out a fishing line now and then. If you do, be sure to get a Nevada fishing license. It costs $7 for a nonresident one-day license and $2 for each consecutive day, which makes for fairly expensive fishing unless you catch lots of them. A year-long license for a nonresident under the age of sixteen costs just $5, however, so if you have a youngster who loves to fish, you'll save money on groceries.

You can grill your catch of the day, roast marshmallows, swim, read books, and go into Las Vegas only when you feel in need of bright lights. If you like more active water sports, you can follow the designated underwater scuba trail at Boulder Beach. Or you might want to rent Jet Skis or a kayak at one of the six marinas on the lake.

Since anyone who can drive a car can navigate a houseboat, you might want to explore some of the lake's coves and crannies, such as the Bat Caves and Lower Granite Gorge on the Colorado River.

Even if you haven't hired a houseboat, that shouldn't stop you from enjoying Lake Mead's special places and pleasures. Boulder Beach is a two-mile stretch popular for sunning and swimming. Sandy Point is another favorite spot for swimming and fishing. And if you want to get your share of striped and largemouth bass, black crappie, bluegill, channel catfish, and trout to cook over a campfire, all you have to do is buy a fishing license and rent a boat at one of the marinas.

For daytime sightseeing, Lake Mead Cruises (702-293-6180) has departures daily from Lake Mead Resort Marina. Although they cost $14.50 for adults and $6 for children, two-for-one coupons are often available in the free weekly magazines.

The Past Revisited

One of the best museums around, the Clark County Heritage Museum, features both indoor and outdoor exhibits on twenty acres of land. Centerpiece of the museum is the relocated Boulder City Railroad Depot from Hoover Dam construction days.

Inside the depot, exhibits range from fossils of prehistoric sea life and dinosaurs to a display focusing on the history of neon in Las Vegas. Outside on Heritage Street, historic buildings include the Giles/Barcus House, built in the mining camp of Goldfield around the turn of the century and moved to Las Vegas in the 1950s, where it served in turn as a residence and a retail store.

There's also a replica of a nineteenth-century newspaper office on Heritage Street, complete with early-day presses and other equipment. Several pieces of railroad rolling stock, including a shiny black locomotive, are on display near the museum's entrance, and an interpretive trail leading to a re-created ghost town winds through displays of antique mining equipment.

Special exhibits at the museum, such as "Heritage Toyland, 1900–1959," "Ribs, Rods, and Splits: Appalachian Oak Basketry," and "Las Vegas History of Entertainment" are presented throughout the year. Open from 9 A.M. to 4:30 P.M. daily, admission is $1.50 for adults, $1 for children. The museum is located between Henderson and Boulder City just off the Boulder Highway (702-455-7955). This museum keeps getting better every year.

Down by the Riverside

About fifteen years ago, there was only one casino at Laughlin, ninety minutes southeast of Las Vegas. Now, a neon strip of nine major gambling halls stretches along the Colorado River, with homes, condos, shopping centers, and a golf course in the hills behind them.

Laughlin is a laid-back sort of place, favored by seniors in winter and families in the summer. Hotel/casino rooms and meals are even cheaper than in Las Vegas. Recreational vehicles may be parked free for three days at a time in casino parking lots, so some RVers stay all winter, moving from lot to lot.

Highlights include walks along the river promenade and rides on the free shuttle boats that ply the Colorado. There are free entertainments throughout the year, too, such as Sunday tea dances at the Riverside, a December talent show put on by casino employees, and fishing tournaments with cash prizes.

At nearby Lake Mojave National Recreation Area, rangers lead free walks through the desert and to the petroglyphs in Grapevine Canyon. There are also free guided tours of Davis Dam, and water sports as well as fishing on the lake itself.

To reach Laughlin, take the Boulder Highway (Highway 95), being careful not to miss the left turn at Railroad Pass where Highway 93 splits off from Highway 95. Turn left on Highway 163 to Laughlin. For a more scenic (and time-consuming) route, turn off Highway 95 just south of Searchlight and travel the dirt road through Christmas Tree pass, where it's not unusual to see piñion pine trees decorated with holiday ornaments. This is ooh-and-aah country, with spectacular granite outcroppings and giant boulders stacked on top of each other. Don't forget your camera.

Digger's Delight

Some 125 years or so ago, prospectors began tramping around Nevada Territory, looking for gold, silver, and other minerals to make them rich. In the years that followed, hundreds of mining camps sprung up, several of them in the area around Las Vegas. In the mountains twenty-nine miles southwest of Las Vegas is Potosi, the state's oldest lode mine. Goodsprings, thirty-five miles southwest of Las Vegas, was a booming mining camp that produced lead and zinc at the turn of the century. Now it's a rock hound's paradise. Other mining camps include Sandy, thirteen miles west of Goodsprings, and Eldorado Canyon, forty miles southwest of Las Vegas.

Poking around old mining camps isn't for everyone and can be downright dangerous if you don't use good sense and stay away from abandoned mine shafts and posted areas. But it's great fun if you're like a lot of Nevadans who enjoy searching for buried treasure in the form of old bottles and other artifacts of bygone days (they say digging around old outhouse sites is best since that's where people threw things they didn't want any longer).

In All Directions

If you have more time, there are still other excursions you might make. At Nellis Air Force Base, north of the city, you can visit the home of the Thunderbirds, the USAF aerial demonstration team. The ninety-minute free tour includes a film showing the team in action, a walk through the Thunderbird Museum, and a visit to the hangar where an F-16 is on display. Tours are conducted on Tuesday and Thursday, beginning at two P.M. (702-652-4018).

Floyd Lamb State Park, known to the locals as Tule Springs, is the place close to Las Vegas where you can commune with nature, watching birds in a natural habitat of two lakes with clumps of tules (cattails) growing in them. You'll see commoners such as ducks, geese, starlings, and blackbirds as well as the more exotic peacocks and heron.

And if you just happen to have brought your motorcycle along, you'll want to hrmphhhhhhhh-hrmphhhhhh-hrmphhhhhh to Nellis Sand Dunes, just twenty miles northwest of the Strip.

Nevada's only winery, Pahrump Valley Vineyards, offers tours of its mission-style complex from 10 A.M. to 4:30 P.M., followed by complimentary wine tasting. On Saturday nights from mid-June to mid-October, the winery also presents "Free Concerts on the Green," with programs running the musical gamut from Broadway show tunes to hot blues.

To get to Pahrump, one of the state's foremost agricultural areas and a retirement mecca for ex-Californians, take U.S. 15 south from Las Vegas and turn right on State Highway 160. The trip takes about an hour.

Pahrump is big on celebrations. If you catch the annual Harvest Festival and Rodeo in mid-September, Cinco de Mayo (Fifth of May), or festive Fourth of July celebrations, you're in for a small-town treat.

For an excursion tacked onto an excursion, take the Tecopa Hot Springs turnoff off State Route 160 at Pahrump. Five miles from the junction, the HIDDEN HILLS RANCH–CATHEDRAL CANYON sign marks the gravel road leading to your destination. Cathedral Canyon is a natural canyon that has been enlarged, remodeled, and enhanced with walkways, an artificial waterfall, a stairway chiseled from the rock leading down to the canyon floor, and alcoves in the walls. Focal point of the cathedral is a huge statue of Christ, and art from around the world decorates the walls. Built by a former Las Vegas district attorney, the canyon is open to the public and admission is free.

Tips on Touring

If you want to see the Las Vegas countryside but driving is out of the question, you'll find a variety of commercial tours available.

By and large, they're expensive. But that doesn't mean you necessarily have to pay full price. By checking through all the free weekly publications, airline in-flights, and coupon racks at the Convention Center and tourist centers on the Strip, you're bound to find discount coupons for many of them. The depth of the discounts is quite consistent year-round.

A Word of Caution

Whenever you go on any extended hikes at Red Rock Canyon or other Nevada semiwilderness areas, it's a good idea to let someone, such as a park ranger, know where you're going. Always carry water. Since temperatures plummet at higher elevations after the sun goes down, consider carrying along a windbreaker, too. And remember that rattlesnakes, scorpions, and Gila monsters make their home in various parts of southern Nevada, so watch where you walk and what you touch, especially when you're in rocky places or sandstone areas with crevices.

8

Getting Around

Ever get home from a trip and wonder where all the money went? Though we budget for the major expenses—airfare or gasoline, accommodations, entertainment, and dining, we rarely consider the "little" expenses that add up to big bucks. One of these little expenses that's among the easiest to control in Las Vegas is the cost of getting from place to place.

The first transportation you'll need, if you're like most of the 42 percent of Las Vegas visitors who arrive by plane, will be from McCarran International Airport to your hotel or motel.

A taxi will cost you $8.50–$12.50 to the south Strip (Excalibur, Luxor, Tropicana, San Remo, MGM Grand, and other lodging places in that area); $12–$14 to the center Strip (Flamingo Hilton, Mirage, Treasure Island, and Caesars Palace, and the neighboring properties); $18–$20 to the north Strip (Riviera, Stardust, Frontier, Westward Ho, and Circus Circus); and $18 to $20 downtown. These rates, when shared by four people, don't amount to so much. But if one person's paying the tab plus the tip, it can close to equal what he or she would pay for a day's car rental.

When you're laden with luggage, however, there's only one other option—hotel shuttle service—unless you choose to rent a car, since very few properties provide free airport transportation. Two companies, Bell Trans and Gray Line, offer van service to the major hotels. Bell Trans charges $3.50 per person to the Strip and $4.75 to downtown, while Gray Line's Strip rate is 25¢

less and the downtown rate the same. You can save $1 on the Strip fare and $1.05 downtown by buying round-trip tickets from Gray Line.

A couple of features I've found objectionable about airport shuttle vans is that there's little legroom and some of the vehicles seem to have badly worn shock absorbers. If there are two or more of you plus lots of luggage, therefore, it may not be worth the savings to take the shuttle—especially if you have a bad back. However, if you're alone, it could be your most economical option.

We briefly discussed the city bus system, CAT (Citizens Area Transit), in chapter 2. When you're traveling with luggage that can fit on your lap and/or on the floor by your feet, you can take a CAT bus (302 to the Strip, 109 to downtown) for $1. Youth from the ages of five to seventeen, seniors, and people with disabilities ride for 50¢.

The buses are clean and theoretically run every thirty minutes, though this can vary from a longer interval to one that's much shorter. The buses and shuttles usually take about the same amount of time to make their trips since, while the bus stops more frequently, its stops are of shorter duration as there's no luggage loading and unloading.

If there are four or more people in your party, auto rental is frequently the very best way to go, as far as both convenience and cost are concerned. Even if you're alone, you may want to rent a car for a day or two. Major agencies in Las Vegas, most of which have toll-free numbers, include:

Agency Rent-A-Car	800-321-1972
Alamo	800-327-9633
Allstate Car Rental	800-634-6186
Avis Rent A Car	800-831-2847
Budget Car & Truck Rental	800-527-0700
Dollar Rent-A-Car	800-800-4000
Enterprise Rent-A-Car	800-325-8007

Hertz	800-654-3131
Lloyd's International Rent A Car	800-654-7037
National Car Rental	800-CAR-RENT
Payless Car Rental	800-PAYLESS
Rebel Rent-A-Car	800-372-1981
Thrifty Car Rental	800-367-2277
Value Rent-A-Car	800-GO-VALUE

In addition, there are dozens of other operations. One of the best known is RentAWreck (702-736-0040), which specializes in used-car rentals.

The cost of car rentals can vary so widely—not only from season to season but also from one rental agency to another—that it pays to shop around. When we phoned the major agencies for January and June 1996, rates on their least-expensive cars, the prices ranged from $16 to $39.95 a day in January, $14.99 to $29.99 in June. Both the high and low January prices were for Ford's Aspire model, while the Hyundai Accent and Ford Aspire were available at June's low and while the highest price was for four models, including Toyota Corolla and Honda Civic. Weekly rates went from $99.99 to $159.99 during January and June, with both rates for Aspires.

Ask a number of questions when you're phoning the agencies. Of course, you'll want to know if any discounts are available, but there's other information that is even more important. For example, at least one company charges an 8 percent airport fee of all customers who arrive at their office via airport shuttle. Others give unlimited mileage only to California, Nevada, and Arizona residents. There may be booking requirements for the lowest rates, such as making the reservation a day or more in advance; charges for additional drivers; driving-in-Nevada-only stipulations; or drop-off charges if you want to pick the car up at your hotel and turn it in at the airport.

You'll want to check the information you gather against the prices you've seen quoted in newspaper travel and entertainment sections, airline in-flight magazines, and any discount coupons you may have collected via the mail. You'll almost always find a number of $10 off coupons, some of which specify that they're good on any of the company's rental cars. When the coupons can be applied on an advertised special that's competitively priced, you'll have found yourself a winning combination.

One of the best deals I've seen for short-term rentals was offered in 1996 by Value Rent-a-Car. A 99¢ per hour rate with a minimum rental time of one hour had to be booked 24 hours in advance, but included unlimited mileage. In sum, one could rent a car for six hours, drive around town or 350 to 400 miles in the surrounding area and it would only cost $5.94 plus gas. Cars included the Hyundai Accent and comparables.

When you find the best rate, reserve the car immediately. Since rental rates go up with demand, they change almost as quickly as hotel-room prices do.

As a general rule, car rentals are at their very lowest the two weeks before Christmas and at their very highest in January during Comdex and at other times large conventions are in town.

If you're going to be in Las Vegas at the same time a big convention or trade show is taking place, you might not be able to rent any car unless you reserve months in advance. Although you may be able to get an auto club or AARP discount on a car if you can find one to rent, it's doubtful that you will get any better deal than a 5 or 10 percent discount on the company's highest rate.

By contrast, if your visit coincides with a slow or even moderately busy time of the year, you can profit by using either of the two following techniques:

1. Lock in your reservation as far in advance as you can. Two weeks or even two days before departure, phone again the half dozen companies that quoted the lowest rates when you called the first time. See if their rates have changed. If they have, make a new reservation and cancel the old one.

2. Wait until you get to Las Vegas to arrange for the car. Since so much of the action is on the Strip, you may find that you don't need a car all of the time. Perhaps you'll decide to rent a car for only one or two days. If so, you'll have time to check out the weekly magazines and other sources for the best discounts. After you've decided which deals are best, start phoning around for availability. One word of caution—don't call too many non-toll-free numbers if you're doing your research from a pay telephone or you'll spend all your savings in quarters to feed the phone.

The plan that works best for me if I am going to be in Las Vegas for three or four days is a combination of techniques 1 and 2. I check airline in-flight magazines for coupons (you can usually obtain them from the airlines by calling their toll-free numbers) and then phone to reserve a car for the first twenty-four hours of my visit. I make sure that I can pick up the car at the airport and drop it off at one of the company's hotel locations on the Strip without additional charges.

After checking out all the Las Vegas sources for car-rental discount coupons, I reserve another car for the final twenty-four hours of my stay. I pick the car up on the Strip and return it to the agency's airport location in time to catch my plane home. It's always a good idea to allow an extra half hour if the agency is not in the terminal and requires a shuttle ride.

The Lay of the Land

Las Vegas is a relatively easy town to drive in during nonrush hours, although the traffic is very fast on the major arterials, especially those going east/west, such as Tropicana. Streets are generally well marked, however, and if you have a halfway decent map, you shouldn't have any trouble navigating. I like the free bus-route map from CAT best because, although it doesn't include outlying areas, the print is big enough that you can read it at a glance.

The city is laid out on a grid, although four principal thoroughfares—U.S. Highway 95 (a freeway running through town), Fremont Street (which becomes Boulder Highway and joins Highway 95 a few miles out of town), Rancho Boulevard, and part of Las Vegas Boulevard—run diagonally.

When you're driving, you'll soon become familiar with Tropicana, Flamingo, Desert Inn, Sahara, and Charleston, which run east/west and Maryland Parkway and Eastern, north/south, since they're major streets you'll use to get around most efficiently.

Rules of the Las Vegas Road

Now that we've covered the transportation choices and the city's layout, let's talk about specifics.

If you plan to travel to Las Vegas by car, obtain a map in advance (see chapter 12, "Sources and Resources"). Unlike hotels in most cities, Las Vegas hotel/casinos offer free parking—in itself a great savings. Valet parking, which requires only a $1 or $2 tip each time you have your car brought to you, is a good value, especially for women traveling alone.

Even though you have a car at your disposal, at times you might choose to take other transportation.

In Las Vegas, taxi travel is especially expensive for two reasons. First of all, the city is spread out over an area of 84.272 square miles (219.1 square kilometers). Secondly, many of the streets are congested at peak periods. The most heavily traveled road of them all is the Strip. On weekends, and busy weekdays as well, it can look like a slowly moving parking lot from midmorning to midnight.

The streets downtown also suffer from bumper-to-bumper syndrome. Traffic on the arterials running off the Strip is always heavy at rush hour, and since the opening of MGM Grand in late 1993, Tropicana Avenue to the airport, always a busy street, has become even worse.

Keeping all this in mind, you'll realize why Rule No. 1 for

saving money on Las Vegas transportation is: Never take a taxi during daytime unless you have four people sharing or have no other alternative.

Rule No. 2 is: If at all possible, avoid taking taxis to get from one end of the Strip to the other. Las Vegas taxi rates start at a base of $2.20, with an additional 30¢ every fifth of a mile. But one thing the posted rates don't tell you is that the time also ticks away on taximeters. As a result, when taxis are caught in traffic, you pay a lot more than the posted rates.

Case in point: One day I was running late, so decided to take a cab from Luxor,' at the south end of the Strip, to the Riviera, which is about two miles north. It was noon on a weekday during one of the city's slowest times of the year. Ten minutes later, when we had traveled less than a mile, the meter read $4.90. By the time we reached the Riviera, it was $10. And that didn't include the tip.

When I asked the driver why he hadn't detoured around the Strip, he replied that taxi drivers can get in trouble if they don't take passengers to their destinations by the shortest route. Therefore, whenever you're forced by circumstances to use a cab from one point on the Strip to another, tell the driver you want him to take the least-expensive route.

In my book, a taxi ride along the Strip is a winner for only one reason: if there are four or five people in your party to share costs, and you want to consider it as after-dark entertainment, catch a cab on a busy night and spend your ride oohing and aahing at the lights (it's said that the electricity used by the Mirage alone in twenty-four hours would light Nevada's capital, Carson City, for twice that length of time).

Cabs are often impractical, too, for transportation to off-the-Strip attractions, because of the time/distance constraints mentioned above. Certainly, there may be times when the only way to get to where you want to go is by taxi, but even then, you can save money by timing your trips so they don't coincide with rush hours. You will also want to use a taxi when you're going off the Strip after dark, especially if you are traveling alone.

A Ticket to Ride

Fortunately, Las Vegas has an excellent bus system as far as tourist needs are concerned. With twenty-nine routes, buses travel to—or near to—almost all the city's points of interest.

The fare for buses that go up and down the Strip is $1.50. Fares for all other buses are $1 and 50¢, with exact change required. Transfers, which must be used within the hour, enable you to get on the bus at your hotel or motel, transfer to a second bus, and reach attractions that would have cost ten to twenty times the cost of your ticket if you had traveled by cab.

To save even more money, you can purchase a bag of forty individual 50¢ tokens (called CAT coins) at the CAT customer service window of the Downtown Transportation Center for $15 a bag and save 25 percent over the cash fare. Even if there are only two of you, you're apt to take public transportation twenty times in the course of a four-day visit. Even if you don't, you can save any coins you have left over for another visit, since they aren't dated.

The buses you use most often will be those plying the Strip and going between the Strip and downtown. Most first-time Las Vegas visitors are surprised at the length of the Strip. They may have heard that it's three miles long, but it is only when they start walking from one casino to the next that they realize how long that three miles can be.

It doesn't matter if you don't take the bus back in Dallas or Cincinnati or Newport, at least give the CAT buses a chance. On your first ride, grab a "System Map and Guide to Services" and the "Time Schedule and Map Book" from the rack at the front of the bus. The former features the large, easy-to-understand map of all the routes that was mentioned earlier in the chapter, plus fare information. The latter devotes two pages (including a small map) to each individual route. You can also obtain these publications in advance by writing CAT (see chapter 12, "Sources and Resources").

Before you set out to visit an attraction, study the time

schedule/map booklet to see which route will get you there most efficiently. You can also get information from the bus drivers, especially if the bus isn't crowded. Since we feel that bus travel is the best way for most people to get around Las Vegas, we've included route information whenever possible in the chapters on attractions and sightseeing.

Trolleys and Shuttles

In addition to the CAT buses, trolleys go up and down the Strip, stopping at each of the major hotel/casinos along the way. Since the fare is the same, $1.20, the trolleys offer the advantage of your not having to walk to the bus stop. The disadvantages are a rougher ride and not-so-frequent service, since they run every thirty minutes as opposed to the ten- or fifteen-minute intervals between buses.

There's a downtown trolley, too, which goes down Fremont, Main, Stewart, and Ogden streets and costs 50¢ for adults, and 25¢ for youths five to seventeen years, seniors sixty-five and older, and people with disabilities. The trolley operates daily except Thanksgiving, Christmas, and New Year's Day from 7:30 A.M. to 11 P.M.

Several casinos offer free shuttle service that you may want to use. In most cases, the reason behind these free rides is that the sponsoring organization owns both the properties that are linked by the transportation. In others, they're devices to create goodwill and lure customers to one or more casinos. The shuttles currently in operation include:

♦ A tram between the Mirage and Treasure Island. While the Mirage entrance is at the front of the hotel, you have to walk through the casino at the Treasure Island end. However, even at that, it's a good deal shorter than the walk along the Strip.

♦ A monorail between Excalibur and Luxor. Expect a rather long walk through both casinos on this one, which makes it almost a toss-up with walking the entire distance outside.

◆   A shuttle between the Palace Station (on W. Sahara), Fashion Show Mall (between Treasure Island and the Frontier Hotel/Casino in the center Strip area) and Metz Plaza (between MGM Grand and the Aladdin near the southern end of the Strip) runs every half hour from 9 A.M. to 11 P.M.

◆   A shuttle between the Barbary Coast (north of the Flamingo Hilton on the center Strip) to Gold Coast, downtown, runs continuously from 9:30 A.M. to 12:30 A.M.

◆   A shuttle between Sam's Town, on the Boulder Highway, and the Stardust (north strip) runs every four hours.

◆   A shuttle between the Rio Suite Hotel on W. Flamingo Road and Caesars (center Strip) runs every half hour from 10 A.M. to 11 P.M.

◆   A monorail from Bally's to MGM Grand runs continuously, 9 A.M. to 1 A.M.

In All Directions

If you've never been to Las Vegas, the next piece of advice may perhaps strike you as bizarre. But take it on faith, because it involves getting around with as little wear and tear on yourself as possible.

Whenever you go into any of the big hotel/casinos, head straight for the hotel concierge or bell desk and ask for a map of the property (it helps if everyone in your party gets one). Then, if you split up to gamble and plan to regroup later at a certain spot, you'll all be able to find the rendezvous point without problems.

You see, some of the casinos are gigantic (the biggest of them all, MGM Grand, is seventeen-thousand square feet—the size of ten average houses). There are slot carousels by the megascore, multiple gaming pits and keno lounges, all of which look amazingly alike. Add to this the fact that casinos have no windows you can look out of for clues to your location.

Also, the flashing, blinking, and revolving lights plus miscellaneous sounds of music, slot-machine burbles, loudspeaker messages, and general crowd noise can cause major disorientation. As a result, you can wander in circles, just as you might if you were lost in the wilderness. Even if you're by yourself without any deadlines to meet, it will save you frustration if you have a map to find your way when you decide to leave.

Pedal Pushing

If you've brought your bike along, it will serve you well when you visit such places as Red Rock Canyon and Valley of Fire or ride around Las Vegas' residential areas. There are, however, almost no bike paths within the city limits, so you should be prepared for traffic if you attempt to ride on the main city streets.

Renting a bike is a rather expensive proposition. The going rate is $20 for a half day, $26 for a full day, and $90 a week. One couple who wanted to bicycle but didn't care to pay those rates bought two used bikes at a thrift shop, then sold them at a secondhand store when they were getting ready to leave for home. A great idea unless you aren't able to sell the bikes.

Pedestrian Power

So far we haven't mentioned the least expensive of all transportation modes—walking. Las Vegas is made for pedestrians since it's flat as any city you'll find. And even though the area is large, attractions are generally within walking distance—sometimes a long hike, but viable for people who are used to walking a few miles a day.

It's important, however, for walkers to realize that Las Vegas is like other big cities with a large transient population. Some areas aren't places where you really ought to go walking, especially by yourself. And it can be dangerous to wander off the beaten path at night. The Strip, however, is considered to be safe twenty-four hours a day if you take customary precautions such as carrying wallets in inside pockets, hanging on securely to purses (or better yet, not carrying them), and not wearing a good deal of expensive jewelry.

Also remember that Las Vegas is in the desert, so humidity is generally less than most visitors are accustomed to. As a result, your body can lose a lot of liquids without your being conscious of the loss. Be sure to drink plenty of nonalcoholic fluids anytime of the year, and especially during the summer months. You'll probably want to wear a hat and slather on the sunscreen then, too, as well as taking your walks in the morning and evening.

Putting on the Ritz

Now that we've finished talking about the least-expensive ways to get around, let's talk about the most. As promised in the table of contents, here's the lowdown on limos.

Presidential (702-731-5577) charges $65 an hour for a superstretch limousine, complete with bar stocked with glasses, ice, and soft drinks; a complimentary bottle of champagne; color TV, VCR, and stereo; a rose for each lady; and the driver in a tuxedo.

If you can be content with a regular stretch limo, without the roses, champagne, and bar, settle for Bell Trans (702-385-5466), which has the lowest prices in town—$33 an hour for six- and eight-passenger stretch limousines.

9

♠

Strictly for Seniors

Some people say that because of Las Vegas' low prices, there aren't a lot of discounts for seniors. Those people just haven't looked around.

Because there *are* savings—10 percent here, 5 percent there—that can add up to substantial amounts. Granted, you may find out about them in unusual places. They're often advertised on casino marquees and in newspaper and weekly magazine ads, where you would expect them to be. But you also will find senior specials announced on signs in the windows of business places, on freestanding signs in shopping strips, or even on small placards at the checkout counters of chain stores.

But let's begin at the beginning. You should start to think about senior savings when you are planning your trip—figuring out how you'll get to Las Vegas and where you will stay.

When you're comparing airfares, you'll find that each of the major airlines has two types of promotions for seniors over the age of sixty-two. These programs are virtually identical, no matter which airline sponsors them. One type of program features coupon books to be used for multiple trips by the same person. The other offers discounts on individual fares.

When you're planning to take more than one trip by air during a twelve-month period, you might consider buying the senior coupon book. These books are available in four-coupon amounts, and currently cost about $540, with each coupon equivalent to a one-way ticket. United, American, and Delta are among the airlines serving Las Vegas that have these programs. It's necessary to make reservations fourteen days in advance, but there are no periods during the year when the coupons cannot be used.

The second program entitles travelers over the age of sixty-two to 10 percent off the price of all published fares. Best of all, the person who's sixty-two can bring along a companion of any age at the same fare—even if it's a five-year-old grandchild.

As far as accommodations are concerned, you won't find that many of the major hotel/casinos cater to seniors with special rates. But those that do are worth finding out about.

The Hilton hotels—and there are two of them in Las Vegas—have what is called the Senior HHonors Program. For people sixty years and over, the plan discounts room rates up to 50 percent, gives 20 percent discounts on dinner at hotel restaurants, provides a free daily newspaper, free health-club privileges (where available), and special check-in and check-out—including late checkout—arrangements. Annual domestic membership is $50. Hilton guarantees its Senior HHonors room rates are lower than those given to AARP members.

Harrah's offers seniors 20 percent off room rates, based on availability. Regular midweek rates at Harrah's range from $50 to $149. Another quality hotel, Bally's, has a special senior rate of $63 plus tax that's good any time of the year, based on availability. Alexis Park offers a senior rate (also based on availability) on its least-expensive suite of $65, rather than $135 regular rate.

It's a good idea to check the senior rates against any packages a hotel might be offering, to see which will be the better deal for you. Bally's, for purposes of illustration, also offers a midweek package to the general public for $178, which includes two nights' lodgings plus brunch, two tickets to their production show, "Jubilee" (tickets regularly sell for $42 and it's a spectacular show), $76 per person off on health spa admission, taxes, and gratuities.

At the Four Queens, Club 55 offers all sorts of perks to

senior travelers, via a social club for slot players over fifty-five. Membership is free and benefits include discounts on rooms, food, beverages, and gift-shop purchases. Club members can also attend free monthly bingo sessions, dances, parties, lectures, and slot classes.

Just by signing up for the club before you register at the hotel desk, slot-club personnel say, you'll get rooms that are regularly $47 during midweek and $57 weekends for $39.95 and $48.45. As you accumulate points by playing the casino's slot machines, you start acquiring scrip to use for discounts on food and such.

The room rate you'll be entitled to on subsequent visits to the hotel depends upon your point total, which in turn depends upon how many coins you put into the machines. While this is a good deal for people who plan to spend a lot of time playing slot machines and want to stay downtown, it's not for nongamblers except for the initial room discount.

Several Las Vegas motels also offer senior discounts, among them Day's Inn Downtown (707 E. Fremont Street, 702-388-1400); Econo-Lodge Downtown (520 S. Casino Center Boulevard, 702-384-8211); Fairfield Inn by Marriott (3850 Paradise Road, 702-791-0899); Comfort Inn South (5075 S. Koval Lane, 702-736-3600); Best Western Parkview Inn (905 Las Vegas Boulevard N., 702-385-1213); Blair House Hotel (344 E. Desert Inn Road, 702-792-2222); Town Hall Casino Hotel (4155 Koval Lane, 800-634-6541); and Center Strip Travelodge (3419 Las Vegas Boulevard S., 702-734-6801).

But perhaps you would prefer taking a packaged tour. Grand Circle Travel (347 Congress Street, Boston, MA 02210, 800-221-2610) and Saga International Holidays, Ltd. (222 Berkeley Street, Boston, MA 02116; 800-343-0273) have tours especially geared to seniors. While they may not cost less, certain features may fit in with your needs and personal travel style better than those of tours that are available to the general public.

Elderhostel is another option for seniors. Some years sessions are held on the campus of the University of Nevada, Las

Vegas and last a week. Others are conducted on two or more sites. For example, in 1996 "Ancient Images in the Rocks" and "Water Color" were just two of the topics studied during a two-week course which combined one week in Las Vegas and one on the shores of the Colorado River. The $770 fee included all meals, accommodations and classes.

Packing Procedures

When you're packing, you'll want to remember to put any medications you may be taking into your carry-on luggage, along with copies of the prescriptions. If these medications need refrigeration, you should notify personnel at the hotel so that you can have the use of a small refrigerator.

Travelers of all ages can take comfort in the fact that there's a twenty-four-hour medical clinic on the Strip. Called Doctors on Call (DOC), the walk-in clinic is located on the eighth floor of the Imperial Palace Hotel (702-735-3600) and provides free shuttle service.

Once You're There

You'll find that getting around town is not only easy, but cheap, with 50¢ fares for anyone who is sixty-five or older. Bus drivers don't check identification, so you can probably fudge on this one—if your hair is graying and your conscience allows it.

People with handicaps are also charged 50¢ and all buses are equipped to handle wheelchairs. It's also stated on signs in the buses that people are to give up their seats to those who require them. Bus stops along the Strip are sheltered and contain two or three benches, a real boon when you want to rest or wait for friends.

Dining Discounts

Most casino restaurants rely on their low-priced food specials and buffets to bring people, including seniors, into the casino and don't offer any discounts other than those that people of all ages can use. There are, however, occasional exceptions. The Gold Strike Inn, for example, charges seniors only $1.99 at its buffet on Wednesday night (all other adults must pay the regular price).

Among the restaurant chains, Denny's offers a senior menu, while Carl's Jr. gives a 10 percent discount, Sizzler gives 20 percent, Shoney's offers 50¢ off on most items. Other restaurants—including some of the best—advertise with senior discount coupons in the weekly magazines. For instance, Alpine Village Inn offers a 10 percent discount on food to diners over the age of fifty-five.

Seniors, especially, should be on the lookout for spur-of-the-moment specials. They're usually announced in the newspapers. For example, a few weeks after MGM Grand Adventure theme park opened and attendance failed to reach anticipated levels, people over the age of 59 were admitted free of charge. While these deals don't go on indefinitely, they're great while they last.

As you noticed in chapters 5 and 7, the majority of museums as well as some other attractions offer discounts to seniors. Often these are half-price and well worth taking advantage of. At some of these attractions, you'll need to produce your driver's license or other proof of age. Sad to say, when an attraction with special admissions for seniors also offers discount coupons, they usually don't apply to the senior prices.

Frequently, free or low-cost events take place that appeal especially to seniors. For instance, "Big Band Dance Parties," featuring music from the thirties, forties and fifties, are held every now and then at Arizona Charlie's. There's no cover charge or minimum at these early-evening affairs.

Biggest event of the year especially for seniors is the Salute to Seniors, held the first part of February. Sponsored by the Nate Mack Lodge of B'nai B'rith, the two-day event features exhibit booths, prize drawings, dancing, and big-name entertainment. Admission is free.

Senior centers located in various parts of the city also welcome visitors and offer educational programs and ongoing classes such as ceramics, painting, quilting, and sittercize (exercises you can do while remaining seated).

Local seniors report that two of the best senior centers are Dula Senior Complex (450 E. Bonanza Road, 702-229-6454), which is open Monday through Friday, 9 A.M.–10 P.M., Saturday, 9 A.M.–5:00 P.M., and Sunday, 11 A.M.–4 P.M.; and Derfelt Senior Center (3333 W. Washington Avenue in Lorenzi Park, 702-229-6601), which is open Monday through Friday, 8 A.M.–4 P.M.

Seniors can get first-class exercise at cut-rate prices in Las Vegas, too. Several golf courses, including North Las Vegas Municipal Golf Course (daily) and Black Mountain Country Club (Monday and Thursday) offer senior rates. Senior guest passes, good for use of all of the Bennett YMCA facilities for the entire day, regularly cost $5, but on Friday they're $3. The Y is at 4141 Meadows Lane, right across from Meadows Mall, so the easiest way to get there is by taking the mall trolley from downtown.

Three Las Vegas publications especially for seniors contain information about activities. They are *Prime Magazine* (702-871-6780), available at grocery and convenience stores; *Senior Spectrum* (702-792-3963), available at two hundred distribution points, including supermarkets and drugstores; and *Nevada Senior Times/Senior World* (702-367-6709), available at senior centers, selected restaurants, and bingo parlors.

While these publications are great information sources, they're even more valuable as a source of discount coupons, since they apply not only to tourist-oriented items, but also toward things like prescriptions, haircuts, and having the car washed.

Mature Traveler (P.O. Box 50400, Reno, NV 89513), a newsletter for seniors, keeps track of new deals for seniors in Las Vegas as well as the rest of the world. The magazine costs $29.95 for a year's subscription and $5 for a single issue, but—

and here's the bargain—you can get a sample copy for just $2. Request one with Las Vegas information in it.

Buying Power

Merchants know that hundreds of thousands of Las Vegas visitors are seniors who winter in the Southwest. They also know that shopping is a leading recreational activity with retirees. So whenever you're in shopping malls or other shopping centers, keep your eyes peeled for senior-friendly signs.

In addition, many of the major businesses have senior programs, providing discounts throughout the week or only on certain days. The following are two stores that give discounts.

Store	Day of Week	Percent Discount
Pay Less (pharmacy only)	Daily	10
Woolworth	Tuesday	10

If you're looking for a specific type of merchandise, check the yellow pages of the Sprint/Central Telephone–Nevada phone book. Advertisers who wish to be identified as giving senior discounts are designated by stars.

An effective technique for saving money on larger purchases—those over $100—when they're made in small business places is to ask the manager if there is a discount when you pay in cash rather than by credit card.

Since the manager is eager to make the sale, chances are that he or she will knock off the percent that the store has to pay the credit-card company. It isn't a lot, but even 2 or 3 percent makes a difference. Although anyone can use this technique, it seems to work best for seniors—especially those who look as if they might have retired from operating a small business.

Be on the lookout, too, for senior discounts on services such as those offered by barbershops and beauty salons. You're most likely to find them during November, December, and

January, when business is generally slowest and lots of "snow-birds" are in town.

Senior Sightseeing Savings

Even if you don't see senior-discount information on tour-company advertisements, be sure to ask if there are any. Frequently, these discounts are available, but it is necessary to ask for them.

In chapter 7, we talked briefly about Laughlin, the riverside gambling strip southeast of Las Vegas. Of all the sightseeing tours, the Laughlin junket is the one you shouldn't miss. Prices are so low that it's cheaper to take a tour than to drive. Furthermore, Laughlin is the most senior-friendly place around (an estimated 70 percent of its winter visitors are in the over-sixty age group).

Some dozen companies operate Laughlin tours. They're all approximately ten hours in length. You spend about two hours in transit each way and five and a half to six hours in Laughlin.

To my mind, three of the best values are those that follow:

The Gray Line tour (702-384-1234) includes lunch at either the Riverside or Golden Nugget plus discount/gaming coupons. The tour costs $6.95 for two people with a freebie magazine coupon. Upon presentation of an AARP membership card, another 10 percent is deducted, making the total cost $3.14 per person.

Discount Grand Canyon Sightseeing's tour (702-383-8592) is free for two people (with coupon) and includes lunch in the cheery Flagship Buffet of the Laughlin Flamingo Hilton, a free drink, and funbook for each person.

Guaranteed Tours (702-739-9585) costs a whopping $10 for two people with a coupon, but includes a free buffet lunch at the Edgewater and funbooks. In addition, participants get free tickets to the "Viva Las Vegas" show at the Sands, and two-for-one tickets to the "Country Tonite" show at the Aladdin.

Non-neon Options

Here's a sampling of things to do in Laughlin that will make your six hours there memorable, even if you don't spend any time at the tables.

♦ Ride the free shuttle boats that ply the Colorado. Boats go between the Riverside, Edgewater, Colorado Belle, and Pioneer casinos and parking lots on the Arizona side. There's also a water-taxi service that goes to all the casinos. You can ride the water taxis all day for $3 ($2 for a single trip between one casino and another).

♦ Take a shuttle-bus tour of Casino Row for $1.50 (exact change required). The price is the same whether you go from one casino to the next (definitely not a deal unless your feet are tired) or if you stay on board while the shuttle covers the entire route which includes residential Laughlin. Buses run every fifteen minutes day and night.

♦ Walk along the Colorado on the wide promenade that extends from the Edgewater to the Riverside, a distance of half a mile. Benches line the walkway, which is lighted at night.

♦ Hop aboard the Ramada Express, the miniature train pulled by Old Number 7 that takes passengers between the front of the hotel and the parking lot. Scenic it's not. But it's free.

♦ Stop, look, and listen to the free casino entertainment, which ranges from the unmemorable to well-known Big Tiny Little, who appears frequently in the Colorado Belle's Riverboat Lounge. You might also want to browse around in the shops on the Belle's mezzanine.

◆   Check out the bargains at the new Laughlin Horizon Factory Outlet Center across Casino Row from the Flamingo Hilton. Among the 50 or so stores are Mikasa, Guess, Polo, Ralph Lauren and Big Dog Sportswear. There's a food court, too.

◆   Admire the 60 vehicles at the Riverside's Classic Car Collection where admission is free. Stars of the auto show include a 1938 Packard Model 1605 formerly owned by Juan Peron and a 1931 Rolls-Royce Imperial Cabriolet.

◆   Stroll around Mexican-themed Harrah's Del Rio, perhaps the most colorful casino on the Row, with its interior designed to look like a south-of-the-border village. If you feel like playing video poker, Harrah's has a group of machines located so you can look out on the river while you play. It's a great place to sit with a free drink.

Whenever sightseeing tours based in Las Vegas interest you, be sure to ask a number of questions before paying any money. Find out if there will be any additional costs; whether you will be picked up at your hotel and delivered back to it when the tour is over; and how long you will stay at each of the stops on the tour (you might also ask if you will stop at each of the points along the route or merely drive by some of them).

Settling Down

Since the early 1980s, southern Nevada has become one of the leading sunbelt retirement destinations, with more than 88,000 retired persons living in the area at last count. While that might not seem like a lot of people in the more populous states, in one with less than 1.5 million residents, it's a significant figure.

Many of the retirees have come from California, but ex-residents of all the other states have also been attracted by the wealth of facilities, entertainment options, and, of course, the climate. Additional incentives are the absence of state income and state estate taxes.

If you're visiting Las Vegas with an eye to choosing it for your retirement home, you'll want to visit the Chamber of Commerce (711 E. Desert Inn Road, 702-735-1616) to obtain information. "Here Is Las Vegas," one of the publications you will receive, contains extensive information on real estate, city government, attractions, events, medical services, and other facilities.

10
♠

Family Fun

"Family fun" is often a euphemism for doing what the kids want. But Las Vegas offers a wealth of attractions that both youngsters and their parents can participate in—without a whimper from anyone.

Now, I realize that while Las Vegas has been known by a good many names—Sin City, The World's Entertainment Capital, America's Number One Vacations Destination—it has never been touted as a great place to take the kids. Until recently. With the advent in the early 1990s of mega-resorts geared to family vacations, the city has taken on a whole new dimension.

It's a place where you *could* spend a lot of money entertaining the children, but it doesn't have to be that way. Many of the activities that appeal to youngsters are free; others are low cost.

The price of accommodations, as you've seen in chapter 3, is as reasonable as you'll find in any metropolitan area, and the choice is varied enough to suit any family. The five hotel/casinos briefly described below are among those that are especially appealing to families.

Treasure Island gets my vote for the most creative exterior of any Las Vegas hotel/casino. Instead of a plain old sidewalk along the Strip, pedestrians walk along a gangway with rope-rigged railings. Next to the gangway two ships—a pirate galleon, *Hispañola*, and a British Navy frigate, HMS *Britannia*—lie at anchor on a moatlike body of water. On the other side of the water, the casino's facade has been designed as a seaside settlement with windows and balconies overlooking the water. Every hour and a half, starting at 3 P.M. until 10:30 P.M. the two ships battle and the pirates always win.

The free show itself is reason enough for kids to want to stay at Treasure Island, but the hotel also has a kid-pleasing ambience throughout, with murals of pirates and their booty, ships' mastheads, and a generally swashbuckling decor.

Treasure Island's central location is one of the best on the Strip since it's an easy walk to several other hotels that have attractions suitable for children. The only drawback is that its rates are higher than most. However, during slow times of the year, rates can drop as low as $49. Children under twelve in the same room with parents stay free. There's a charge of $10 per child for those over twelve.

If I were a kid again, I would also long to stay at Excalibur. With an exterior of turrets and towers, a moat, and a drawbridge, it's every child's idea of a medieval castle. Inside, the theme is carried out with banners, heraldic shields, strolling minstrels, jugglers, and jesters.

On the lower level, carnival games have a medieval twist. My favorite is a horse race, with each player sitting at a long counter facing the racecourse. When the signal is given, each player rolls a ball into holes with various point values, with each successful toss moving a knight in armor and his steed forward in the race. The player whose knight reaches the finish line first wins.

There's also an afternoon show (Saturday–Thursday, 2 P.M.) featuring the royal Lipizzaner stallions ($7.95) at Excalibur, which kids like a lot. Hotel rates at Excalibur go from $39 to $69 Sunday through Thursday, $89–$103 Friday and Saturday. Children under eighteen stay free.

Circus Circus, Las Vegas' first family hotel/casino, came into being about twenty-five years ago. It's still wildly popular—and with good reason. The midway is the main draw with carnival games, food stands, and funhouse mirrors. Top-drawer circus acts perform in the ring every day from 11 A.M. until

midnight (performers—especially those with school-age children—consider Circus Circus jobs among the best in the world
since they don't have to keep moving around). The most
attractive feature, as far as many families are concerned, is the
room rates, which start as low as $39 a night for up to four
people in a room.

MGM Grand Hotel, Casino & Theme Park is a destination in
itself. And considering that, it can be a terrific bargain if you're
able to visit during December or January, but not right around
the holidays. In the relatively slow December/January period,
room rates are at their lowest ($59–$69; children under 12, free;
over 12, $10). Theme park admission isn't currently charged,
but there are charges for the major attractions.

The MGM Grand Adventures theme park, Las Vegas' first,
covers thirty-three acres with its streets themed for cities and
areas in different parts of the world—Casablanca Plaza, New
Orleans Street, Tumbleweed Gulch, and six others. Craft shops
and restaurants line the streets, which lead to seven rides and
five theater shows.

The Lightning Bolt ride is an indoor roller coaster, housed
in a four-story building filled with lights and sounds that
simulate a space voyage. Dugout canoes roll through a winding
river that plunges from heights of from twenty-five to forty feet.
Deep Earth Exploration (a motion simulator) appears to plunge
its explorers into the center of the earth—right in the middle of
a lava flow. Backlot River Tour takes boat passengers through
different movie sets demonstrating how films are made. Other
rides include Grand Canyon Rapids (a raft ride), Parisian Taxis
(bumper cars), and the Haunted Mine.

Among the theater shows, "The Magic Screen" is a musical
revue that combines live entertainment, film, and special
effects. "You're in the Movies" takes selected spectators and
transforms them into stars, putting them in costumes and
electronically superimposing on them pre-filmed personalities.
In addition to the theater shows, entertainers such as MGM's
mascot lion; Dorothy, Scarecrow, Tin Man, and Cowardly Lion

from *Wizard of Oz*, and troupes of dancers and musicians add to what park publicists call its "Grandmosphere."

Tropicana Resort. Though this is definitely a hotel/casino designed for adults, kids love it, too. Especially those who practically live in the water. The 425-foot walkway between the two hotel towers, lined with macaws, toucans, and parrots, is a good place from which to get an overall view of the grounds.

There are fish ponds, thirty waterfalls, three outdoor spas, and three swimming pools, along with a wonderful water slide. Carvings of two Maori gods that weigh 300,000 pounds each and stand 350 feet tall dominate the outer island, with jungle sounds and island music adding to the tropical ambience. In summer there's free entertainment outside and a laser light show twice nightly.

Rates vary with availability from $59 to $229 (children under eighteen stay free if no additional beds are required), so it's a good idea to book early for rooms during traditionally busy times of the year. A deterrent to reserving rooms at the Trop is the long wait on the toll-free line, during which you're subjected to tedious commercials in a Caribbean accent.

Although virtually all Las Vegas hotels and motels have swimming pools, they're outdoors. This means that it can be mighty chilly swimming from November through March (some of the pools are closed during this period). If you're planning to visit Las Vegas during the winter months with children whose idea of a perfect vacation includes hours in the pool, your best accommodation bets are those where the pool is sheltered, such as the Golden Nugget. Indoor pools at UNLV and the Bennett YMCA (see chapter 9, "Strictly for Seniors!") are open to the public at certain hours year-round.

A number of restaurants, too, appeal especially to children. Sherwood Forest Cafe in Excalibur has a children's menu, and the decorations in the Pirate-themed buffet at Treasure Island are fun for youngsters to look at.

Fortunately, most of the free and two-for-one food you can get with coupons rates high with kids. Though the coupons can be redeemed only by people over twenty-one, there's nothing to say who eats the hot dogs or hamburgers. This means that there really is such a thing as a free lunch—every day of their vacation—for families who like fast food.

There are times, when traveling with young children, that extreme measures are in order—like ordering dinner from room service. When the kiddies are so tired you're uncertain whether they are going to eat or throw a tantrum, the privacy of your hotel room can be a bargain. The extra money you spend can be saved the next day when everyone is rested.

Picnics, too—especially at a park where the children can run around letting off steam—save both money and sanity. If you don't have a car, take the bus to Sunset Park (Sunset and Eastern avenues) and eat your sandwiches there. And bring a Frisbee if you have one, because there's an eighteen-hole Frisbee golf course at the park.

You'll also save money if you can bring snacks from home to last the whole trip, rather than shoving quarters into vending machines with their overpriced wares. One family I know has their children carry two favorite toys or games plus snacks in their backpacks whenever they go on a trip. Additional snacks are brought by the adults in their carry-on bags for flights or in the trunk when they travel by car.

Show-and-Tell: What I Did on My Vacation

Although we've told you about the free pirate show at Treasure Island, The Royal Lipizanner Stallions, the Circus Circus midway, and MGM Grand Adventures, there are scads of other places to which kids will beg and plead to be taken. Doing them all will result in a depleted bankroll and the cranky, exhausted children mentioned above. Our suggestion for saving money is that you do the free and low-cost activities that appeal to you first, then choose among the others in accordance with your budget and available time.

The "Funbook Game"

Since kids, like adults, get a kick out of getting something for nothing, on the day you visit Circus Circus, you can have some extra entertainment with free funbooks. The following works best if there's at least one adult for each child.

1. Before you go to Circus Circus, stop at Slots-A-Fun, which is right next door. People at the entrance of Slots-A-Fun hand out Silver City funbooks to adults leaving the casino. Have each of the adults in your party go inside and come out again to obtain one of these coupon books.

2. Walk across the street and about a block south to Silver City to redeem the coupons. Among them are one for free popcorn and a certificate for a free Circus Circus gift—usually a hat or a fanny-pack.

3. Of course, to get the gifts you have to go back to Circus Circus. But since that was where you were headed in the first place and the kids are happily munching popcorn, there will be no complaints. After all, the youngsters know whose heads will wear the hats and waists those fanny-packs will be buckled around!

Other great freebies you might want to collect while you're in the area are the foot-long hot dogs, which are free with coupons from the Westward Ho funbook (be sure to grab a supply of paper napkins and a plastic knife from the serving counter so you can cut these huge hot dogs into manageable portions).

While some children will want to spend a long time watching the White Tiger Habitat at Mirage, others will get restless after just a few minutes. That's no problem, because it's free and there are lots of other things to see and do nearby, such as the Treasure Island pirate fight.

There's also the Live Dolphin Display at Mirage. A $14-million, 1.5-million-gallon pool of man-made seawater provides the habitat for five dolphins. Spectators can watch them frolic and being fed from both aboveground and underwater viewing areas. Admission is $3; children under three years, free. Hours are eleven A.M. to seven P.M. (702-791-7111).

More mammals, reptiles, and other creatures live at Southern Nevada Zoological Park (1775 N. Rancho Drive, 702-648-5955). Though exotics like Bengal tigers and Barbary apes roam around, many visitors find that its more interesting residents are animals indigenous to the Southwest, such as coyotes, raccoons, badgers, lizards, and desert tortoises. Open nine A.M. to five P.M. daily except major holidays, admission is $5 for adults and $3 for seniors and children two to twelve years.

At Lied Discovery Children's Museum (833 N. Las Vegas Boulevard), kids can crawl through Toddler Towers, tap a tune with their toes on the Musical Pathway, and create color computer prints. They can pilot the Space Shuttle and play disc jockey. This first-rate museum features more than a hundred hands-on exhibits and has many special programs throughout the year. Best of all, they let adults play, too. Don't miss this one even if you don't visit another attraction that charges admission. Open Tuesday and Thursday-Saturday, 10 A.M.–5 P.M.; Wednesday, 10 a.m.–7 P.M.; Sunday, 12–5 P.M. Closed Monday. $5, adults; $4, students and seniors; $3, children three to eleven; two and under, free (702-382-3445).

The Las Vegas Natural History Museum (across the street from the Lied at 900 Las Vegas Boulevard N., 702-384-3466) isn't as slick as its neighbor, but it's an interesting museum nonetheless. One reason is the animated dinosaurs, which make all sorts of horrific noises (it won't be unusual, however, if your little ones don't like them a bit).

Small sharks swim in a three-hundred-gallon tank, and there's a hands-on children's room where they can touch fossils, bones, and all sorts of nifty stuff. When you visit the museum, be sure to bring along one of their brochures for each child so that they can receive a free gift at the museum gift shop and science store. Admission to the museum is $5 for adults; $4 for students, seniors, and military; $2.50 for children four to twelve.

The Magic and Movie Hall of Fame at O'Sheas Casino (3555 Las Vegas Blvd. S.; 702-737-1343) displays what is advertised as a "multi-million- dollar exhibit of magic, movie and ventriloquist memorabilia." Admission is $4.95 for adults and $3 for children 12 and under. Although it's open Wednesday through Sunday from 10 A.M. to 6 P.M., best time to visit is in the afternoon, since mini magic shows at 2, 3, and 4 P.M. are included in the admission price.

Throughout the year, special events such as Halloween haunted houses, a children's festival at Sunset Park, and free jazz, bluegrass, and country concerts downtown are put on under the auspices of the Clark County Parks and Recreation Department (702-455-8200). The Clark County Library (702-733-7810) and Allied Arts Council (702-731-5417) also sponsor entertainment that's fun for the whole family.

Be on the lookout, too, for the family-oriented benefits put on by various organizations. At one of them, the Festival of Trees and Lights, fifty decorated trees, a gingerbread village, professional entertainment, and music by local choirs are only the beginning. Children get to decorate their own gingerbread cookies, shop at a "kids only" gift shop, and make holiday crafts, too—all for just $3 for adults, $2 for seniors, and $1 for children over the age of three.

A good place to find out about family entertainment is in the free publication called *Las Vegas Kidz*, distributed all over town.

The only ice-skating rink in Las Vegas is at the Santa Fe

Hotel (702-658-4991). Admission is $5.50 for adults, $4.50 for children, including skate rental. Sessions last two hours, except on Saturday and Sunday afternoons, when they're three hours. On Friday and Saturday nights, the Las Vegas Aces hockey team plays at the rink from October through March. And don't be surprised if you see Nicole Bobek, 1995 U.S. Ladies Figure Skating Champion, doing some triple jumps. Bobek, who owns a home in Las Vegas, trains at the Santa Fe when he's in town.

Roller skating at the two Crystal Palace rinks in Las Vegas (4740 S. Decatur Boulevard, 702-253-9832) and (3901 N. Rancho Drive, 702-645-4892) costs $5, including skates. Tuesday night, however, is family night, when families of four or less can skate for a total of $10.

If you plan a family outing to Red Rock Canyon, stop at the visitors center for the combination guide/workbook that describes the half-mile Children's Discovery Trail's nine marked sites. Children are asked to do certain things when they're walking the trail, such as looking at the plants, smelling the pine tree's bark, and listening to the creek, in order to learn more about their environment.

The Foxtail Snow Play Area, just off the Lee Canyon Road at Mt. Charleston, is the area's best spot for wintertime sledding, tobogganing, and inner-tubing. There are rest rooms, tables, and grills nearby as well.

Not So Cheap Thrills

Anyone who has ever taken a youngster to a video arcade realizes how quickly quarters can disappear. But given a chance, the kids I know would choose playing arcade games over most other entertainments. Following are some of the bigger video operations on the Strip.

Atari Adventure Centers (at Caesars Palace and the Riviera Hotel) each offer more than fifty games ranging from standards like Pac-Man to prototypes of new video games. At Bally's–Las Vegas, the arcade features air-hockey, carnival, and video games.

Cyber Station in the Forum Shops features still more arcade games.

The Flamingo Hotel funbook contains a coupon for four free plays in the hotel's game arcade. Adults can redeem only one coupon for four free game tokens per day, but there's nothing that says you can't stockpile the tokens and let the children use them all in a single visit to the arcade.

Several other coupons in the Flamingo Hilton funbook work well for families—two-for-one hamburgers; a six-inch submarine sandwich for 99¢ with the purchase of one that's a foot long; buy one scoop of Baskin-Robbins ice cream and get a second scoop for 50¢; buy one slice of pizza, get the second for $1; free fries with any purchase at Burger King.

Wet 'n Wild (on the Strip just south of the Sahara) features twenty-six acres of water-related activities. There's the half-million-gallon Surf Lagoon with ocean-size waves and a thrill ride called Banzai-Banzai. The Bomb Bay drops people feet first from a big capsule into the water. Willy-Willy sends them spinning round and round at over ten miles an hour. Other water rides include the Black Hole, the Raging Rapids, White-water Slideways, and the Blue Niagara.

Though children under nine or ten years of age find the water-park concept exciting, many of them are scared—and some actually terrified—of going down the big slides. They'll probably prefer floating around on the Lazy River and/or spending their time in the Children's Water Playground, with its mini-size water slides, water cannons, and bouncing Lily Pads.

The water park is open from early May through September. Summer hours (first part of June through the first part of September) are 9 A.M.–9 P.M. All-day tickets cost $15.95 for children from three to nine years, $29.95 for everyone who's older. Season passes cost $85, and seniors pay half the adult admission.

Several discounts have been available from time to time, including $2 off daily admission, $3 off daily admission after three P.M., and two-day children's admission tickets for $6 off the price of regular admission for two days. Some discounts, such as the $2-off coupon available at selected car-rental agencies, are in effect all season long. Others vary with the time of year. April, May, and September are the months during which the deepest discounts are generally given.

Grand Slam Canyon at Circus Circus (702-734-0410, extension 5218). This five-acre indoor amusement park, which is climate-controlled, features 140-foot sandstone cliffs, tunnels, grottoes, and a waterfall. Star of the park's attractions is the Canyon Blaster, the only double-loop, double-corkscrew indoor roller coaster in the United States. The Rim Runner, a water-flume ride, careens down a mountain and through a tunnel before it splashes to a stop. The Twist and Shout is a raft ride through twisting tubes. Hot Shots involves playing laser tag in a futuristic environment. Children under forty-eight inches in height can't take the Canyon Blaster, while there's a forty-two-inch height minimum for the other attractions. Admission of $4 includes one major ride. One day before Christmas, 1993, two tins of canned goods was the admission price.

Omnimax Theatre at Caesars Palace is a giant domed movie house with screens surrounding the theater. Viewers are propelled into space, under the sea with the sharks, high above the Rockies, or through time itself. Since some of the shows can be frightening, the management suggests parental discretion. Hourly screenings are held from two to ten P.M. daily, except on Friday and Saturday, when they're from one to eleven P.M. Admission is $6, adults; $4, seniors, children two to twelve, physically challenged, and military personnel.

Guinness World of Records Museum (2780 Las Vegas Boulevard, a few hundred feet north of Circus Circus behind Arby's, 702-792-3766), isn't for everyone, but some children like it a lot. The museum features replicas of record holders, such as the world's bestselling cookie (Oreo) and longest-necked woman (15.7 inches). The Guinness jukebox plays record-breaking songs that have made music history, and an array of data banks dispenses information on world-record facts and figures. Admission is $4.95 for adults; $3.95 for students, military, and seniors; $2.95, children under twelve; but you can find $1-off coupons quite easily. Merlin's Magic Motion Rides at Excalibur each offer a three-minute visual experience—of riding a runaway train, a roller coaster, or a bobsled. Each ride costs $2. Open from ten A.M. to one A.M., 702-597-7777.

Sometimes youngsters aren't as bedazzled by Las Vegas glitter as they are with traditional amusements such as those at Scandia Family Fun Center (paralleling the west side of I-15 at 2900 Sirius Avenue; 702-364-0700.

The mini-structures on the miniature golf course ($5.50 per player) are based upon Scandinavian buildings and include a medieval castle, a lighthouse, church, and windmill. There are bumper boats and raceway cars ($3.95), arcade games and batting cages. $14.95 buys an "Unlimited Wristband," good for all activities for one day. The "Super Saver," which includes one round of golf, two rides, and five arcade tokens, costs $10.95.

Bonnie Springs/Old Nevada (1 Gunfighter Lane, Bonnie Springs in the Red Rock Canyon area, 702-875-4191) is a western fun town with shoot-outs, shops for browsing, souvenir shops. If you have never been to a re-created western-town amusement before, you might consider driving out, but don't expect a Knott's Berry Farm sort of place. Admission is $6.50 for adults, $5.50 for seniors, and $4 for children.

The Strip After Dark

Don't be surprised if sometime years from now your children tell you that the best part of the family's vacation in Las Vegas was looking at the lights on the Strip at night. Whether you drive down the three-mile neon extravaganza or walk along only a portion of it, you can be sure that the youngsters—and adults, too—will be enthralled. If you choose to go on foot, take a bus to the center portion of the Strip where the lights are most dazzling and you can see the volcano in front of the Mirage erupt. The spectacular display occurs every fifteen minutes after dark except in inclement weather.

Children are permitted to attend a number of casino shows and certain performances of others if accompanied by an adult. Several of the productions, such as "Country Tonite" at the Aladdin and the pricey "Siegfried & Roy" at Mirage, are definitely appropriate.

Whether you would find some of the others suitable for your children is definitely an individual matter. We do recommend, therefore, that you find out as much as you can about a show—from reading about it, looking at photos in ads, and talking to people who have seen it—before you decide to take the youngsters. Since prices are often $20 or more, unless it's family-type entertainment, younger children will probably have a better time if the money is spent for attractions and activities such as MGM Grand Adventures and Wet 'n Wild.

When the kids get tired of hanging out with Mom and Dad and you haven't brought along a babysitter from home, there are a number of other child care alternative—most of them expensive. For instance, you might phone the guest services desk at your hotel to arrange for a sitter to come to your room. There are also several licensed and bonded services that you can call directly to make arrangements.

Vegas Valley Babysitters (702-871-5161) and Children's Babysitting Service (CBS) at 702-255-5955 or 258-1048 both offer 24-hour hotel in-room service. Vegas Valley Babysitters' four-hour minimum is $37 plus $7 for each additional hour. CBS has a per-hour charge of $8 for one child (50¢ for each additional child) with a four-hour minimum.

Another option is to drop the youngsters off at the new Kids Quest operations where they can have fun with the Playano (playing tunes by walking on its giant keys), work on putting together a puzzle wall and get involved in lots of other exciting activities (see Chapter 13 for more information).

For free baby-sitting, go to the Showboat, Gold Coast, or Sam's Town casinos where they'll watch children two to eight years old for three hours. Two requirements, though—children have to be out of diapers and parents must stay on the premises the entire time.

If you're reluctant to leave your children with strangers, consider bringing along your sitter from home if there's room in the car. Or better yet, talk another family into vacationing in Las Vegas at the same time you do. Then trade evening baby-sitting a couple of nights.

After you're back home with a photo album full of memories, you'll realize that Las Vegas is a repeat-performance sort of place. So don't be surprised if the kids start asking, "Can we go there again next year?"

11

When Is a Bargain Not One?

Okay, we've talked for ten chapters about bargains. But we haven't said a word yet about nonbargains—the offers that make you think you're getting a good deal when you really may not be. Now's the time.

These faux bargains usually fall into two categories, the come-on and the twofer. The come-ons are generally in the form of gambling coupons, but they can also be coupons for a certain amount or percentage off purchases in selected stores and restaurants. These coupons can be helpful if you're planning to play the table games, buy meals at the buffets or restaurants, and purchase certain items in the stores anyway, but they're not bargains if they inveigle you into parting with cash for doubtful benefit.

The twofer has even more popular appeal. We all have friends who will buy almost anything—whether they need it or not—because they can get two for the price of one. In Las Vegas, this kind of shopper is in bargain-hunter heaven.

This is not to say that two-for-one offers can't be great deals. It's just that they're bargains only so long as you need or really want what you're buying, if the quality of the product is reasonable, and if the "one" part of the equation isn't overpriced to make up for the "two."

There's a third kind of coupon that you won't see quite as

often. It's the "buy this and you'll get that, too." These can be either real money savers or money spenders, depending upon a person's practicality quotient.

Let me explain. You've allocated $30 for gifts to bring home to Aunt Marge, your best friend, and the neighbor who's looking after the cat. Among your coupons is one that gives you a free pound of divinity if you buy two pounds of fudge. You ask to sample both candies. They taste great and cost $9.95 a pound, so you take advantage of the offer. You now have gifts for everyone on your list and have spent only $19.90—a savings of $10.10 from your budgeted amount.

Now, let's look at it another way. You buy the candy for $19.90, then realize that Aunt Marge is the only person on your list who will be happy with the candy since your best friend is a health fanatic and your neighbor just went on a diet. They would like T-shirts, though, so you use the coupon that gives you a free poster with the purchase of two T-shirts for $10.95 each. After totaling up the cost of the gifts, you realize that you're $11.80 over budget and have a poster plus two extra pounds of fudge to pack home.

I know this can happen because the same sort of thing has happened to me. What we will do in this chapter, therefore, is to put the microscope to various Las Vegas "bargains," so that it won't happen to you.

Getting Down to Basics

Let's look, in turn, at the basic ingredients of a typical Las Vegas vacation—accommodations, food, attractions and entertainment, getting around, shopping/souvenirs, sightseeing, and gambling—from the bargain vs. nonbargain perspective. After we've examined each of them in turn, I think you'll agree that sometimes it doesn't pay to save money and that sometimes you save money by paying more.

Accommodations. First of all, in examining any hotel/motel room rate for its bargain potential, we have to keep in mind that almost every guest room in Las Vegas is a bargain when compared with rooms in other cities. But the big question here is whether a specific room is a bargain as far as your needs and wants are concerned.

Say you're miserable when you don't get your eight hours of sleep each night. If you take a room in an older property where the plumbing broadcasts the news that someone in a room down the hall or upstairs is taking a shower, if you have a motel room with windows facing the Strip, or a room next to the elevator shaft in a busy hotel/casino, it won't be a bargain even if it does cost only $20 a night. Remember, Las Vegas is a twenty-four-hour town, and hotel guests are just as apt to be going to bed at four A.M. as they are at eleven.

If you should get such a room, go immediately to the front desk and ask that you be given accommodations without the defect you've discovered. The problem is, you don't realize it's the elevator that's waking you up until it has happened a few times, and the plumbing noises may not be readily apparent either. You usually have to spend that first sleepless night before you can get the problem resolved.

You can help guard against problems by getting some knowledge of the property in advance. Ask friends for input from their Las Vegas hotel experiences. Look at books like the *AAA Tourguide for California/Nevada* and/or the *Mobil Travel Guide* (California and the West edition) to see how many diamonds (on a scale of none to five) they award various properties.

You may be surprised to find that ratings don't necessarily rise with prices. Another way of helping ensure that your bargain room meets your specifications is to request the kind of room (quiet, with a view, on the ground floor) you want when you make your reservation.

Beware, too, of the "bells and whistles" hotel packages. Ask yourself if you really will use the extras. If you don't like the taste of champagne, rarely gamble, and hate staying up after midnight, the free bottle of bubbly, funbook worth $50 in casino play, and two tickets to the eleven-o'clock cocktail show aren't going to seem like much of a bargain. By way of contrast, the package that includes free airport transportation, $5 off in the hotel's coffee shop, and a complimentary newspaper very well might.

Every so often you'll come across a funbook containing a coupon that gives you one night free if you book a minimum of two weeknights at the hotel. If you find such coupons at the beginning of your Las Vegas trip and haven't come on a package deal or prepaid your entire hotel stay, you may want to check out the hotels making these offers.

Ask to see the type of guest room that applies to the particular offer (the less desirable rooms may be assigned to people taking advantage of this promotion), determine the midweek rates, and find out if space is available. When accommodations are as good as, or even better than, those you have, it may pay you to move. But be sure to give the first hotel enough advance notice that you won't be charged for an extra day.

Be advised that unless you're saving a significant amount, moving around won't be a bargain if the hotels are at opposite ends of the Strip. Paying the taxi fare plus tipping the driver to transport you and tipping bellmen at both hotels can quickly eat up your profit. This ploy is most valuable when you're unhappy with the hotel you originally arranged to stay in.

During non-peak periods, members of casino slot clubs who have in the past put a sufficient number of coins through the machines get discounted room offers in the mail. The rationale behind these offers is simple—keep the hotel rooms full and count on enough of these slot players to lose enough money to make up the difference and more.

This technique—which masquerades as a bargain—is one only if you are planning a Las Vegas trip anyway and set time limits on how much you can afford in potential losses. A $19 room—even one that ordinarily costs $85—is no bargain when you lose $100 a day in the hotel's casino. Of course, if you should win it's a different story. But that, after all, is what gambling is all about.

Dining. Whether discount food coupons are bargains or not depends upon your food preferences, how much you ordinarily eat, and the ages of the people in your party. If you're a stickler for top ingredients expertly cooked, you will probably want to use only those coupons for restaurants that are known for the quality of their food. Most buffets aren't going to give you a memorable dining experience—at least not in the positive sense.

When you're accustomed to only a cup of coffee and a sweet roll for breakfast, you'll probably not get your money's worth even at an inexpensive buffet. And I've found that buffets in general, unless they cost less than $3, are a waste of money for most children under the age of eight. The kids *take* a lot of food all right, but they *eat* very little of it.

Zero in, instead, on the discounts for single food items such as hamburgers or ice cream cones that you know everyone will like; or those that give you free beverages when you buy a pizza (if that pizza isn't outrageously priced). When you're traveling with a family of teenagers who never seem to get filled up, however, the discount buffets may prove to be your economic salvation.

Lots of different "buy this/get that, too" food coupons are distributed via the various coupon outlets and in funbooks. Some of them are of the frills variety, such as free sake when you order a Japanese dinner or free dessert when you patronize the casino's most expensive restaurant. Others involve regular meal add-ons such as free coleslaw or french fries when you buy a hamburger or other sandwich.

One "buy this/get that" deal gives you free gaming chips if you order the prime-rib dinner at the Four Queens—a bargain if you pocket whatever winnings you get from them. Sometimes, casinos give away deals such as two-for-one buffets or two-for-one dinner coupons when you purchase $6 of bingo cards or buy $20 worth of change at the slot change booth. The latter's a genuine bargain if you don't feel honor-bound to put those quarters into the slot machines. Not quite what the casino had in mind, but....

Free-drink coupons in funbooks can clearly be money savers. The free drinks served to gamblers by cocktail waitresses usually are not. If you want to play the slots, socialize with your friends, and have a couple of free drinks, choose the nickel machines. Your "free" drinks will be a lot cheaper. And remember, you must be over the age of twenty-one to drink alcoholic beverages in Nevada.

Attractions and Entertainment. Almost every commercial attraction and production show in Las Vegas puts out some sort of discount coupon. They are bargains only so long as they don't lure you merely because of the discounted rate. If you have a choice of using a discount coupon for either the dinner or cocktail show, the latter is usually the better bargain, since you'll rarely hear people rave about the food at a dinner show.

Getting Around. The only caveats here are that you must consider the size of your group and the physical stamina of the people in it. When there are four or five people, it can be as economical to take taxis or rent a full-size car as it is to travel by public transportation, especially when you make two or more round-trips by bus during one day.

Bus travel's no bargain, either, when it involves folding and unfolding strollers, climbing up the steps with arthritic knees, or carrying sleeping toddlers. So be realistic about the way you travel from place to place. For most people, a combination of modes—buses when everyone's rested, taxis when they're tired, maybe a rental car one day—becomes the best bargain they can strike.

Sightseeing. Commercial tours to points of interest, even with 10 or 20 percent discounts, may not be bargains, especially when there are two or more of you traveling together. Take tours to Hoover Dam, for example. One tour, which costs $20 for two people (if they have the right coupon) includes a drive by stars' homes, a visit to Ethel M. Chocolate Factory and cactus garden, a movie of the Hoover Dam construction, souvenir-shopping time, lunch, and time to take the government Hoover Dam tour, for which there is an additional charge of $5 per person.

The Deluxe Hoover Dam Tour, offered by Gray Line, includes tours of Cranberry World West, Ethel M's, and Ron Lee's World of Clowns, visits to the Clark County Heritage and Hoover Dam museums (total admission charges $6.50) plus a "lite lunch at the Snackateria." Regular tour price in the off season is $21.60 per adult; $19.10 for seniors and children over 10; $15.60, children 9 and under.

You can see that a very small portion of the tour price goes to pay for lunch and admissions. Here's another example. The Gray Line tour to Red Rock Canyon, which includes a visit to the Nevada State Museum, a Southwestern buffet lunch and narration by the driver/guide about the history of the area as you ride through it, costs $28.50 per person.

Your best bargain is a do-it-yourself version of these tours. Rent a car ($14–$20), but don't bother to seek out the stars' homes as there is not that much to see. Wayne Newton, for example, has built a high wall around his. Just take the free Ethel M. and Cranberry World tours, pay your $1.50 person admission at the Heritage Museum, and $1 suggested donation at the Hoover Dam Museum. Take the Hoover Dam tour for $5 for each adult and have lunch anywhere you please.

Since you've rented the car for twenty-four hours, you may want to drive out to Red Rock Canyon in the afternoon. If there are two of you, tours to Hoover Dam and Red Rock Canyon would have cost you a whopping $100 without discounts. On your own, you're able to do all that sightseeing for about $40, which leaves you $60 for lunch. Savings are much greater than that if your party includes three to five people.

Of course, tours are the only way to go for people who cannot or don't want to drive. They're also of great value to people from other countries unaccustomed to getting around in the United States. But be sure to get in on the discounts, since virtually every tour offers them.

Shopping/Souvenirs. Some of us—yours truly included—go a little crazy where money's concerned when we're on vacation. We're more relaxed. Life just doesn't seem so earnest. And those pieces of plastic are very easy to use. Add a handful of dollars-off coupons from shops that look inviting and...goodbye, budget.

The best antidote for these easy-money feelings is to force yourself into periodic reality checks. Would that sweater cost as much back home? Will those snakeskin boots fit into the fashion scene back home in Boston the way they do in Las Vegas? Think about the serape you brought back from Mexico or the monokini you bought on the Riviera. For, after all, Las Vegas is, when compared to some places in the United States, a foreign country.

Gambling. Always remember that *any* offer involving gambling is made with the hope that it will entice you to keep playing. We're talking about the $7-for-$5 bet or double your money back if you win, 50¢ or $1 off on a $3 keno card, $22 worth of poker chips for $20 when you make a buy-in.

You'll read that these gambling coupons give you a .3 or .65 or 1.2 or some such advantage over the house. But that's assuming perfect play and is based on play over an extended period of time. Most Las Vegas visitors are not experienced gamblers and can't be expected to play every hand correctly. Furthermore, the number of coupons you're allowed to play in one casino won't permit you to gamble for very long. You may be very lucky. And then again....

Of course, these coupons are bargains if you plan to play blackjack or keno or poker anyway and if they don't entice you to gamble any more than you originally planned to spend. But if the only reason you play is that you'll get more than the usual amount if you win, it's not only a nonbargain, the affair could turn into a real financial disaster. I've seen this sort of thing happen time and again.

People start out with their $7-for-$5 coupon at the blackjack table (along with the $5 of their own money they have to bet). It's easier to walk away if they win and can pocket the original $5 plus the $7 they've won. But five times out of ten at least, the person who wins on that first hand will keep on playing because winning feels good. If he or she loses that first hand, there's an even greater temptation to risk $5 more in hope of getting the initial $5 back.

And, as we said, that isn't so bad if you've planned to play $5 blackjack. But many people who get caught up in this gambling fever are in reality much happier when they're playing the 5¢ and 25¢ slot machines.

Roulette and Big 6 casino play coupons are never a bargain unless they allow you to play free, and you don't see many of those coupons anymore. The reason they're nonbargains if you have to spend any of your own money is that roulette and Big 6 are the casino games with odds tilted heavily in the house's favor. They are—to be blunt—games for suckers.

Your odds of winning at keno aren't so hot, either, but the free $1 keno ticket with the purchase of a $2 ticket is certainly worth taking advantage of if you're going to play keno regardless.

The most dangerous come-on of all is the one that offers you many dollars' worth of casino play, but gives out the coupons in installments over a period of two or three hours. One such offer gives $5 in slot machine tokens and $5 in chips for table play when you pay a $2 registration fee. An hour later, you can go back to the redemption desk for $10 in slot tokens and a ten-spot keno ticket.

One hour later, it's time to go back for $5 in slot tokens and $5 in table-play chips. The last installment—$10 in slot tokens, $10 in chips—is doled out an hour after that, three hours after the whole process started.

Table-play chips cannot be redeemed for cash. They must be played. Any winnings, however, are given to the players in redeemable casino chips. The odds against cashing in on a ten-spot keno card are slim since the player must catch at least five numbers to get anything back. Chances of each number being called are one in four.

The slot tokens are also of questionable value, since they can be used only in certain machines. This means that the payback percentage on the machines may well be—and usually is—far lower than that of the other machines in the casino.

While these coupons will add to your gambling fund if you plan to spend three hours in that particular casino, they're a nondeal if you don't. After the first half hour, waiting around in a casino without playing is about as exciting as watching your car on the grease rack. So you decide to gamble a little while you're waiting until it's time to go collect the next "free" tokens and chips.

Getting more poker chips than you pay for sounds like a good deal, and it is if you plan to play poker. Getting more than your money's worth of $1 slot plays is a bargain, too. But only if they're tokens that can be played in any dollar machine in the casino.

Too often, these turn out to be tokens that can only be played in certain machines or points given on the meters of a group of "special" machines where prizes are awarded only when the top jackpot combinations are hit. The number of points accumulated on the meter doesn't matter at all except that it allows the player to play longer. I watched one woman who had paid $20 cash for $40 worth of this kind of slot-machine play build her point total up to 364, only to lose it all eventually because she wasn't able to line up a jackpot during all the hours she played before the points finally ground down to zero.

Giveaway drawings are a favorite with casino promotions people. They usually work something like this. Entrants write their names and addresses on blanks provided by the casino and put them in a drum and/or are given entry blanks each time they win a jackpot of more than a certain amount. Drawings may take place once a day, once a week, even hourly. You almost always need to be present to win. Prizes are usually cash in amounts from $50 to $5,000, but may also be items like mink coats and satin jackets. When you're gambling anyway, you might as well participate, especially if you plan to be in the casino at the time the drawing is scheduled to be held. If you have to make a return trip to the casino, you'll want to think twice.

An equally popular way casinos draw people inside is the coupon promotion that entitles the bearer to a free pull on a special slot machine. One of the bigger prizes currently popular in Las Vegas is a free pull on every slot machine in the casino. Among other top prizes may be trips to places like London and Waikiki, automobiles—usually sporty models that look good on display—and cash. Smaller prizes are apt to be three-night stays at the hotel, dinners for two in the gourmet dining rooms, and all manner of caps, T-shirts, and sports bags bearing the casino's name and/or logo.

Is it worth your while to pull the handle? Sure, if the line's not long and you have nothing else to do. People do occasionally win. But keep in mind that on the regular casino four-reel slot machines, your chances of lining up all sevens are about one in 160,000. Slot machines used in these special promotions often have fewer symbols on each reel, making your odds even less favorable.

The absolutely free daily gambling tournaments—those that don't require an entry fee and let you play on metered machines with the goal of racking up the most points—are worth entering and can be lots of fun, unless competition makes you nervous. While most of the daily gambling tournaments are confined to slot machine play, others feature video poker and 21.

Tournaments that call for an entry fee—usually $10 to $25—are generally not bargains. For that entry fee, most competitors get to play only the twenty minutes of their first round. Those who advance to the semifinals play for twenty minutes more, and finalists play an additional twenty-minute round. Hundreds of people enter these tournaments each day, with preliminary rounds of some competitions going on from midmorning to eight P.M.

In another kind of "tournament," players use their own money and the high scorers of the day (those winning the largest jackpots, usually on slots and/or video poker machines) are given additional cash prizes. Usually, you're automatically entered in one of these competitions if you win a good-size jackpot.

Daily tournaments that are the biggest bargains are those like the free slot tournaments held at Bally's, with five money winners each day. Of course, hundreds of hopefuls play in the short sessions held throughout the day, but the prizes of $300, $200, $100, $75, and $50 are enticing. Winners also get to come back to the hotel for a free two-night stay and the chance to win $5,000 in a winners' tournament.

While the chips cannot be redeemed for cash, the winnings resulting from play with them can, which makes the tournaments a good deal even if you don't place among the winners. Also, the dealers are so congenial that the sessions are great fun.

The two- and three-day gambling tournaments, with entry fees from a few hundred to a few thousand dollars, aren't a bargain unless You win a big enough prize to cover your tournament costs, including any gambling losses you may incur while you're not involved in tournament play.

If you plan to spend several hours gambling in one particular casino, it's silly not to join the casino's slot club. The reason is simple: as long as you're going to spend the money, you ought at least to have something for it.

Though experts have figured that $100 worth of coins has to go through the slot machine receptors to earn $1 worth of premiums, with a 90 percent rate of return that $100 goes through the machine several times before it's exhausted. If you've nothing else to do, you can figure out how many times by multiplying $100 by .90, $90 by .90, $81 by .90, and so on.

Those same experts say that eight hours of $1 slot play will get you a free room for two nights at the hotel/casino where you're gambling. Most hotel/casinos also adjust the rate slot-club players will have to pay for their rooms on subsequent visits in accordance with the amount of their slot play. This "casino rate" can be as much as 50 percent off the regular rate.

Beating the Clock

The biggest hazard we cheapskates have to face is that we may become so engrossed in saving money that we don't have enough time left to enjoy ourselves. So we need shortcuts. I follow the timesaving rules below. You might want to try them.

♦   If you haven't researched Las Vegas in advance of your visit or collected any discount coupons, funbooks, and the like through the mail, go to the Las Vegas Convention & Visitors Authority tourist information room (just to the left of the main entrance at 3150 Paradise Road). You might also want to stop at one of the four tourism centers on the Strip.

♦   When you have accumulated your stash of coupons for free and discounted items, segregate them as to type, i.e., dining, admission to attractions, sightseeing as described in chapter 5. Get rid of those you know you won't use. After all, free hot-dog coupons aren't much use to vegetarians, and most of the souvenir key chains are a bunch of junk. If no one in your party gambles, get rid of the gaming coupons, too. The minutes this takes will save you much more time when you start looking through your collection for specific coupons.

♦   Since it's impossible to see and do everything in Las Vegas in a month—let alone three days or a week—prioritize your activities. On the basis of what you've read and heard, make a list of those activities that sound the most interesting in order of their importance to you. Then pull any discount or free coupons that you can use to help pay for them.

If you have a $2-off admission to one of the two attractions you've listed opposite priority No. 5, for example, the discount may determine which of the two you visit. But keep in mind that the lower price has value in making decisions only in case of a toss-up. Don't fall into the trap of doing something just because you have a $2 discount coupon, or missing out on something else because you don't.

◆   Carry your coupons with you at all times. It will cost extra time if you have to make a special trip to redeem a coupon at a place you walked right past the day before.

◆   When a freebie is of questionable value to you, consider the time it will take you to redeem the coupon.

◆   Above all, remember that the ultimate bargain is having a good time.

12

♠

Sources and Resources

The Las Vegas scene continually grows and changes. So much so, in fact, that a new telephone directory comes out every six months.

Dozens of new free and discount offers appear throughout each year, and old offers are withdrawn just as frequently. Room rates change. Restaurants open, then close their doors forever. So what's the bargain hunter to do?

Fortunately, several sources of information remain constant. These are the sources you should contact while you're planning your trip and/or after you arrive in town. If they don't have what you're looking for, they'll most likely lead you to other sources that do.

Planning

Free weekly publications include:

Today (702-385-2737) contains maps of the Strip and downtown; entertainment listings; a rundown of events (includes gaming tourneys); brief descriptions of area attractions; where to go dancing, and where to take children; listings of hotel/casino phone numbers, golf courses, tennis courts, free gaming lessons, places where various casino games such as poker are played, buffets, selected restaurants, and churches; phone numbers for airline reservations, car rental, taxi companies, and the like, plus fire department, weather service, twenty-four-hour clinics, and other emergency numbers; information on tipping; and advertisements, including money-saving coupons.

In a single issue, these coupons included those for a Lady Luck funbook (with foot-long hot dog), Fitzgerald's mug or watch, $3 off "Splash!" at Riviera, $3 off "Improv" at Riviera, Riviera funbook, $1 off Riviera buffet, 10 percent AARP Grayline discount, other excursion discount coupons, Holy Cow! coupon for free tour and beer, $2 discount for "Star Odyssey" at Stardust, Stardust free deck of cards, Vegas World $50 in game play, and Sands funbook.

Tourguide (702-221-5099) contains essentially the same information as *Today* except there is also a section on fine art and performances. In the issues we studied there were fewer discount coupons.

Where To in Las Vegas (702-362-6722) includes sections on buffets; shows; restaurants; where to go bowling; where to play golf, where to buy videos; where to take the children; where to worship; maps; listings of future showroom entertainments; advertisements; but very few discount coupons.

All of these weekly magazines are about five by eight inches in size. Magazine-size weeklies include *Las Vegas Today* (702-221-5000) and *What's On in Las Vegas* (702-891-8811). *Las Vegas Today* features information on showroom entertainment and casino food and contains a TV guide as well as several coupons.

What's On in Las Vegas is the most complete of the free publications, and each issue covers a two-week period. It includes a potpourri of general information; a show guide; fairly extensive information on lounge shows and other nightlife; a calendar of events; columns and feature articles; maps; brief descriptions of museums and exhibits; a department called "For the Seniors"; information for new residents; listings of the various race and sportsbooks, bingo parlors, gaming tournaments, buffets and brunches, current musical performances and art exhibits; a schedule of future entertainments; brief restaurant reviews; lots of advertisements; and freebie/discount coupons.

A third magazine-size weekly, *Showbiz* (702-383-7185), is found primarily in hotel rooms. A good deal of its space is devoted to a television log, but there is information on casino shows and other nighttime entertainment; rules of the casino games; a gaming-tournament calendar; an extensive listing of restaurants; advertisements; and a few coupons.

There are weekly tabloid-size publications as well. They include *Vegas Visitor* (P.O. Box 42249, Las Vegas, NV 89116) and *Showtime* (900 S. Main, Las Vegas, NV 89101), which focus on casino entertainment and buffets/restaurants. As a rule, they don't contain many freebie/discount coupons.

Another free publication, the monthly *Places and Faces*, is especially useful, however, for its maps and good discount coupons.

You'll find these magazines all over town after you arrive, but since they are helpful for advance planning, you might want to request copies from the Las Vegas Convention & Visitors Authority (LVCVA) tourism department and/or the Las Vegas Chamber of Commerce. Their addresses and phone numbers are:

Las Vegas Convention & Visitors Authority
3150 Paradise Road
Las Vegas, NV 89109
702-892-0711

Las Vegas Chamber of Commerce
711 E. Desert Inn Road
Las Vegas, NV 89109
702-735-1616

You can also obtain a wealth of brochures, freebie/discount coupons, an occasional funbook, maps of Las Vegas, and information on various areas of interest by writing these organizations.

In-flight magazines of airlines serving Las Vegas often have ads containing freebie or discount coupons. Especially important are those coupons that give discounts on auto rentals. Prior to your trip, obtain copies of in-flight magazines of airlines that fly to Las Vegas (flying with a particular airline isn't a requirement for use of coupons found in their magazines). Southwest Airline's and Reno Air's in-flights are particularly good coupon sources.

Two other chambers of commerce will be able to give you information as well. They are:

Nevada Black Chamber of Commerce
Box 4850
Las Vegas, NV 89106
702-648-6223

Latin Chamber of Commerce
829 S. Sixth Street
Las Vegas, NV 89101
702-385-7367

The ultimate resource for people who go frequently to Las Vegas for the gambling and the casino entertainment is a monthly publication called the *Las Vegas Advisor*. It costs $5 for a single issue, $45 for a year's subscription with second-class postage, and $50 with first-class postage; Canadian and foreign, $50 U.S. funds. Send check or money order to:

Las Vegas Advisor
Huntington Press
3687 S. Procyon, Suite A
Las Vegas, NV 89103

If you're driving to Las Vegas, you'll want the official Nevada state map. You can get one from the Nevada State Commission on Tourism, Capitol Complex, Carson City, NV 89710-0005; 800-NEVADA-8 or 702-687-3636.

Accommodations

For ratings and basic information about various Las Vegas lodging places, your best sources are the *AAA California/Nevada Tourbook*, available at American Automobile Association offices (free, but available only to members) and the *California and the West Mobil Travel Guide*, available at bookstores and at most public-library reference desks.

The following hotel/casino list with their addresses and toll-free telephone numbers should be helpful in finding out about their rates and any packages they may be offering.

Hotel/Casino	Address	Toll-Free Numbers
Aladdin	3667 Las Vegas Boulevard	800-634-3424
Alexis Park	375 E. Harmon Avenue	800-223-0888
Arizona Charlie's	740 S. Decatur Boulevard	800-342-2695
Bally's Resort	3645 Las Vegas Boulevard S.	800-634-3434
Barbary Coast	3595 Las Vegas Boulevard S.	800-634-6755
Binion's Horseshoe	128 Fremont Street	800-237-6537
Holiday Inn/ Boardwalk	3750 Las Vegas Boulevard S.	800-465-4329
Bourbon Street	120 E. Flamingo Road	800-634-6956
Caesars Palace	3570 Las Vegas Boulevard S.	800-634-6661
California Hotel	First and Ogden	800-634-6255
Circus Circus	2880 Las Vegas Boulevard S.	800-634-3450
Continental Hotel	4100 Paradise Road	800-634-6641

Hotel/Casino	Address	Toll-Free Numbers
Courtyard by Marriott	3275 Paradise Road	800-321-2211
Debbie Reynolds	305 Convention Center Drive	800-633-1777
El Cortez	600 Fremont Street	800-634-6703
Excalibur	3850 Las Vegas Boulevard S.	800-937-7777
Fiesta	2400 N. Rancho Drive	800-731-7333
Fitzgerald's	301 E. Fremont Street	800-274-5825
Flamingo Hilton	3555 Las Vegas Boulevard S.	800-732-2111
Four Queens	202 E. Fremont Street	800-634-6405
Frontier Hotel	3120 Las Vegas Boulevard S.	800-634-6966
Gold Coast	4000 W. Flamingo Road	800-331-5334
Gold Spike	400 E. Ogden	800-634-6703
Golden Gate	111 S. Main Street	800-426-1906
Golden Nugget	129 E. Fremont Street	800-634-3454
Hacienda Hotel	3950 Las Vegas Boulevard S.	800-634-6713
Hard Rock Hotel	4445 Paradise Road	800-473-7625
Harrah's	3475 Las Vegas Boulevard S.	800-427-7247
Holiday Casino	325 E. Flamingo Road	800-634-6765
Holiday Crowne Plaza	4255 S. Paradise Road	800-227-6963
Hotel San Remo	115 E. Tropicana Avenue	800-522-7366

Hotel/Casino	Address	Toll-Free Numbers
Imperial Palace	3535 Las Vegas Boulevard S.	800-634-6441
Jackie Gaughan's Plaza	1 Main Street	800-634-6575
Lady Luck	206 N. Third Street	800-523-9582
Las Vegas Club	18 E. Fremont Street	800-634-6532
Las Vegas Hilton	3000 Paradise Road	800-732-7117
Luxor	3900 Las Vegas Boulevard S.	800-262-4444
Maxim Hotel	160 E. Flamingo Road	800-634-6987
MGM Grand	3799 Las Vegas Boulevard S.	800-929-1111
Mirage	3400 Las Vegas Boulevard S.	800-627-6667
Monte Carlo	3770 Las Vegas Boulevard	800-311-8999
Nevada Palace	5255 Boulder Highway	800-634-6283
New York-New York	Tropicana and Las Vegas Boulevard S.	800-693-6763
Orleans	4500 W. Tropicana	800-331-5334
Palace Station	2411 W. Sahara Avenue	800-634-3101
Quality Inn	4575 Boulder Highway	800-634-6617
Residence Inn by Marriott	3255 Paradise Road	800-331-3131
Rio Suites Hotel	3700 W. Flamingo Road	800-752-9746
Riviera	2901 Las Vegas Boulevard S.	800-634-6753

Hotel/Casino	Address	Toll-Free Numbers
Royal Las Vegas	99 Convention Center Drive	800-634-6118
Sahara	2535 Las Vegas Boulevard S.	800-634-6666
Sam's Town	511 Boulder Highway	800-634-6371
Sands	3355 Las Vegas Boulevard S.	800-634-6901
Santa Fe	4949 N. Rancho Drive	800-872-6823
Sheraton Desert Inn	3145 Las Vegas Boulevard S.	800-634-6906
Showboat	2800 Fremont Street	800-826-2800
Stardust	3000 Las Vegas Boulevard S.	800-634-6757
Stratosphere	2000 Las Vegas Boulevard S.	800-998-6937
Texas	2101 Texas Star Lane	800-654-8888
Treasure Island	3300 Las Vegas Boulevard S.	800-944-7444
Tropicana	3801 Las Vegas Boulevard S.	800-634-4000
Vacation Village	6711 Las Vegas Boulevard S.	800-338-0608
Vegas World	2000 Las Vegas Boulevard S.	800-634-6277
Westward Ho	2900 Las Vegas Boulevard S.	800-634-6651

Travelers with disabilities may want to contact the Nevada Association for the Handicapped (6200 W. Oakey Boulevard, Las

Vegas, NV, 702-870-7050) and Southern Nevada Sightless (1001 N. Bruce Street, Las Vegas, NV 89101, 702-642-0100) for information on accommodations in Las Vegas, although most major properties have rooms that are especially designed and equipped for the disabled.

Dining

There's no single source of objective dining information for the Las Vegas area, so the best way to determine whether you want to eat in a particular restaurant is to (1) look it over and (2) ask to see a copy of the menu. Restaurant write-ups in the weekly publications are almost always about places that advertise in those publications.

For more unbiased appraisals, check out back issues of *Nevada Magazine* for in-depth reviews that are listed in the publication's table of contents. Restaurants are also reviewed in the local newspapers. You'll find these back issues in the periodicals section of the Las Vegas Library at 833 Las Vegas Boulevard N. (702-382-3493).

Attractions, Entertainment, and Sightseeing

Buying the issue of *Nevada Magazine* that's on the newsstands while you're in town is also an excellent way to find out what's going on in town—from special exhibits at art galleries and craft shows to chili cook-offs and symphony orchestra concerts. If you want to subscribe to the magazine, which is published every two months ($14.95 per year; $19.95, foreign), the address is:

Nevada Magazine
1800 Highway 50 E.
Carson City, NV 89710-0005
702-687-5888

In addition to the free weekly/biweekly and monthly magazines listed above, you'll get valuable information by reading the newspapers. They are:

The Las Vegas Review-Journal
P.O. Box 70
Las Vegas, NV 89125
702-383-0400

The Las Vegas Sun
800 S. Valley View
Las Vegas, NV 89107
702-385-3111

The Friday and Saturday editions of the *Las Vegas Review-Journal* are especially useful, since in addition to information they also contain excellent discount coupons, such as two-for-one admissions to King Arthur's Tournament at Excalibur.

For information on specific activities and attractions, you may want to contact the following:

Las Vegas Parks and Recreation Department
2601 E. Sunset Road
Las Vegas, NV 89120
702-455-8200

The people at the recreation department are extremely helpful and can provide you with information about activities, parks, and recreational facilities such as exercise courses, swimming pools, and picnic areas. If they don't have the answers to your questions, they'll tell you where to find them.

The following numbers can be called for information of interest to both residents and tourists:

Sammy Davis Jr. Festival Plaza at Lorenzi Park
702-229-6704

West Las Vegas Art Center 702-229-4800

Charleston Heights Art Center (films, exhibits, chamber music) 702-229-6388

Fern Adair Conservatory of the Arts (musicals, ballet, theater) 702-458-7575

Reed Whipple Cultural Center (concerts, film festivals, melodramas) 702-229-6211

UNLV concerts (music and dance) 702-739-3101

Las Vegas Stars (baseball at Cashman Field) 702-386-7200

Wedding information 702-455-4415

And here are some sightseeing information addresses and phone numbers that may prove useful:

Nevada State Parks:	Nevada Division of State Parks Capitol Complex Carson City, NV 89710 702-687-4384
Mount Charleston:	Toiyabe National Forest 550 E. Charleston Las Vegas, NV 89104 702-222-1597
Red Rock Canyon trails:	Bureau of Land Management Las Vegas District Office P.O. Box 26569 Las Vegas, NV 89126 702-647-5000
Valley of Fire:	Valley of Fire State Park Box 515 Overton, NV 89040 702-397-2088
Lake Mead:	National Park Service Lake Mead National Recreation Area 601 Nevada Highway Boulder City, NV 89005 702-293-8907

The park service will be able to give you information on

such things as campsites and numbers you can call to find out about scuba gear, scuba classes, houseboat rentals, and other Lake Mead activities.

Hunting and fishing: Nevada Department of Wildlife
                          State Mail Complex
                          Las Vegas, NV 89158
                          702-486-5127

There are four tourist centers on the Strip where you can obtain information on attractions and tours as well as pick up brochures and free/discount coupons. They are clearly marked, so you shouldn't have any trouble finding them. You'll find the weekly magazines at transportation company desks on the baggage level at McCarran International Airport, in all the major hotels (usually at the bell or concierge desks), at the Greyhound bus depot downtown, the tourism office at the Las Vegas Convention Center, and in the racks at the Las Vegas Chamber of Commerce.

Getting Around the City by Bus

Copies of the Citizens Area Transit (CAT) system's "Transportation Center System Map and Guide to Services" and "Time Schedule and Map Book" are in racks at the doors to all CAT buses and at the Downtown Transportation Center (DTC), 300 N. Casino Center Boulevard.

They can also be obtained by contacting:

Regional Transportation Commission of Clark County
301 E. Clark Avenue, Suite 300
Las Vegas, NV 89101
702-228-7433

Family Fun

In addition to the information in the weekly magazines, another magazine, called *Las Vegas Kidz* (4082 Aduana Ct., Las Vegas,

NV 89103, 702-252-0404), contains a date-by-date "Things to Do" section. Included are dozens of low- or no-cost programs that children will enjoy, such as candy making, crafts workshops, story hours, and festivals. The magazine is available at 250 distribution centers, including Las Vegas libraries, recreation centers, supermarkets, and other stores.

You might also want to watch community-affairs announcements on KLAS-TV, Channel 8, weekdays between eight and eight-thirty A.M. for organization-sponsored events geared to families, such as ethnic festivals and school carnivals.

Senior Data

The following centers offer ongoing classes and activities for seniors:

Sunrise Community Center
2240 Linn Lane
Las Vegas, NV 89115
702-455-7600

Parkdale Community Center
3200 Ferndale
Las Vegas, NV 89121
702-455-7517

Winchester Community Center
3130 S. McLeod
Las Vegas, NV 89121
702-455-7340

One last suggestion. When you can't seem to find the information you're looking for, phone the reference desk at the Las Vegas Library, 702-382-3493. The people there are skilled at research and are almost sure to be able to answer your questions.

13

♠

Robbing the One-armed Bandits

First of all, let's get one thing straight. The house always wins. Almost.

Gambling is a business. In fact, it's Nevada's number one industry. Just look at the high-rise casinos. They weren't built on customers' winnings.

Sure, you've heard friends brag about their big jackpots. But no one talks much about the money they've lost. So don't be deluded into believing that you're going to go home from Las Vegas with lots of money. Sure, it *might* happen. Chances are, though, it won't.

But that's not to say you can't have fun playing the slots or blackjack or craps *if* you enjoy the excitement and don't have your heart set on being a big winner. Just decide in advance how much money you're willing to risk losing. If you win, great. But don't think that your good luck is going to last forever.

And when you start losing, don't become desperate and keep playing to make up those losses. Most likely, you'll be sending good money after bad. Instead, if Lady Luck abandons you, check chapter 5 to see what non-neon attractions the city has to offer, and take a break from the casinos so you'll have money left to come back and play another day.

That admonition out of the way, let's talk about what you can do to make the most of the gambling money you've decided to spend.

Following the Rules

No one under the age of twenty-one may play at or linger around the slot machines or gaming tables. Minors can pass through casinos on their way to restaurants, hotel rooms, or other nongaming portions of the building, but they cannot stop and watch the action. This state law is strictly enforced.

And although you may think that anything goes in the casinos, cheating definitely doesn't. Frequently, you'll read reports in Nevada newspapers about people being apprehended for slot machine cheating and other schemes meant to defraud the casinos. These crimes are felonies and punishable by prison sentences, so don't try anything that is even the least bit dishonest (like trying to put a foreign coin that's worth a couple of pennies into a quarter slot machine).

Just about every casino in Las Vegas relies on electronic surveillance to spot cheaters. In "the eye in the sky" systems, cameras constantly take pictures throughout the gaming areas, with screens monitored by security twenty-four hours a day.

Even though casinos use cameras, regular folks are forbidden to use their cameras in most of the gambling palaces. In fact, violators can be detained and their film confiscated.

You're also not supposed to take gambling chips or the $1 tokens out of a casino, either. Instead, cash them in before you leave. The tokens will work in gambling machines at other casinos, but you won't be able to play the chips at blackjack or craps tables in other clubs.

The Games Gamblers Play

You will probably read articles about beating the casinos at their own games. Perhaps you've even bought a book on winning at 21 or playing perfect video poker. I won't deny that you can improve your 21 game and that correct play maximizes your chances at video poker (I even wrote a magazine article on the subject).

But if you do decide to augment your knowledge by reading one of the thousands of books that have been written about systems to use in playing everything from video poker and baccarat to craps and 21, keep one thing in mind. It takes time to absorb the material these books contain and to integrate your new knowledge into your play. So, don't buy these books at the eleventh hour and expect to get much out of them. And steer shy of any books that promise to make you a winner playing slot machines. There is no such thing as a winning slot strategy.

It takes a long time to become an expert, so don't expect to become an overnight wonder on the basis of reading the following material. However, most casino games aren't complicated, so if you retain what you read, it should increase your playing time/minimize your losses.

The most entertaining way of learning how to play blackjack, craps, baccarat, and other casino games is to take advantage of the free lessons offered by many of the major properties and some of the smaller ones. Unfortunately, in the last couple of years several casinos have discontinued these sessions and have substituted brochures that explain how to play. Needless to say, reading instructions doesn't take the place of hands-on experience, which in Las Vegas can be very expensive.

Casinos that are currently offering classes include:

Aladdin—Hands-on classes with visual aids in the "College of Higher Gaming Knowledge" are held every Wednesday, Thursday, and Friday, with times and locations posted in the casino; 702-736-0111.

Bally's—Instruction at tables in the casino includes craps, Monday through Friday at 11 A.M. and 3 P.M.; roulette at 10:00 A.M. and 4:30 P.M.; blackjack at 1 P.M.; baccarat at 1:30 P.M.; paigow poker at 2 P.M.; 702-739-4111.

Caesars Palace—Lessons in blackjack, craps, pai gow poker, minibaccarat, and roulette are given to small groups, Monday through Thursday, at tables adjacent to the Olympic

Casino Box Office. Class times vary. Race and sports wagering instruction is offered Wednesdays at 1 P.M.; 702-731-7110.

Circus Circus—Half-hour lessons in roulette, 21, and craps, with morning and afternoon sessions, Monday through Friday, except holidays, in the Main Casino; 702-734-0410.

Flamingo Hilton—Monday through Friday, blackjack classes are held at 10 A.M. and 2 P.M.; craps at noon; poker at 2 P.M.; baccarat at 2:45 P.M.; Caribbean stud at 10:40 A.M.; Double Down and Let 'er Ride, 3 P.M.; roulette at 4 P.M.; 702-733-3111.

Harrah's—Captain Casino gives instruction in roulette, blackjack, craps, baccarat, and pai gow piker every Monday through Friday on the casino floor. Times are posted in the casino; 702-369-5000.

Imperial Palace—On Monday through Thursday in the main casino area, participants use mock chips at classes that are more than an hour long. Times are blackjack, 9 A.M. and 2 P.M.; craps, 11 A.M. and 3 P.M.; 702-731-3311.

Lady Luck—The Casino's "College of Gaming Knowledge" (not to be confused with the Aladdin's "College of Higher Gaming Knowledge") awards diplomas (suitable for framing) in craps, 21, and roulette at the completion of classes held weekdays in the main casino; 702-477-3000.

Las Vegas Hilton—The game fundamentals are taught seven days a week in craps, 10:30 A.M.; roulette, 1:30 P.M.; pai gow poker, noon to 8 P.M.; blackjack, in the learning center; 702-732-5111.

Riviera—Five days a week, the gaming program includes lessons in craps, 10 A.M.; blackjack, 11:15 A.M.; roulette, 12:15 P.M.; baccarat, 1 P.M. Caribbean stud at 2 P.M.; Let it Ride at 2:30 P.M. Poker instruction is offered Monday through Thursday at 2 P.M. in the poker room; 702-734-5110.

Sahara—The basics of craps, 11:30 A.M.; blackjack, 12:30

P.M.; roulette, 1:30, 2:20, and 3 P.M. in the main table area; 702-737-2111.

San Remo—Gaming lessons are in Japanese only. One hour sessions at 3:30, 5, 6:30, and 8 P.M., with free souvenir card deck given to each participant; 702-739-9000.

Stardust—Classes held Monday through Friday from 9 to 10:30 A.M. and 3 to 4 P.M. focus on an overview of all casino games. Instruction from 9 A.M. to 5 P.M. concentrates on craps and blackjack; 702-732-6111.

Since schedules can change, it's a good idea to phone in advance.

While classes covering the basics are important, remember that real-life games are different from those where there's no money at risk. For one thing, the casino managers see that their most congenial dealers preside at the gaming sessions, when, in fact, a good many dealers at the regular tables are downright intimidating.

Secondly, the atmosphere at the training tables is relaxing, with lots of joking and light banter. You'll occasionally find a table in actual play that's fun—and more often, a laid-back game of craps where people are enjoying themselves. But by and large, gambling is dead-serious, white-knuckle time.

Be aware, too, that the game quality of computer poker in all its variations or the spinning reels of the slot machines that come so heartbreakingly close to big win combinations can—like any arcade game—be mesmerizing. And those quarters or tokens you're putting in the slots while the machines enchant you aren't Monopoly money.

A Brief Course for Beginners

The following will give you an idea of how the more popular casino games work. Tips on how to make your money last longer follow the explanation of each game.

Slot Machines

At last count, there were well over one hundred thousand of these one-armed bandits licensed for play in Las Vegas. You'll find them not only in casinos, but in supermarkets, drugstores, and some Laundromats as well. They range in size from the standard table models to what the *Guinness Book of World Records* has certified as the largest slot machine in the world— the seven-by-eight-foot Queen Machine that stands a few feet from the entrance of the Four Queens Casino in Glitter Gulch.

Not so many years ago, all the slot player had to do was insert a coin, pull the handle, look at the middle line to see whether a winning combination had come up, and collect any coins that spilled into the tray below.

Now, although most traditional-style slot machines still have handles, many of them are computerized. They have bars that you can push to activate the reels (most of them have handles as well, since studies found that many gamblers felt they had more "control" of a machine when they pulled the handle). Instead of spitting out the coins, contemporary machines often tally up their total under a readout that says CREDITS, and the player must push a button called COLLECT or CASH OUT in order to retrieve these coins

There are also—in addition to the traditional three-reel machines—machines with four and five horizontal reels. Today's symbols are a far cry from the oranges, plums, and bells that date back to the early days. You'll still find the fruit and bell machines, to be sure, but they've been joined by sevens in various colors (some of them even licked with tongues of fire to show how hot they are); bars with gemstones on them; Olympic gold, silver, and bronze "medals"; hot-air balloons that float up if they stop one space below the payline; "wild" symbols in a variety of guises; and logos of the various casinos, which, when lined up in a row, mean the club's superjackpots.

The machines make slurping noises, play tunes when winning combinations are hit. Some of them even talk to the players, though their vocabularies are limited.

As far as the play is concerned, the most important difference in today's machines is that more likely than not they have multiple paylines (ways in which winning combinations can occur). When the newer machines have a single payline, they require that multiple coins be played in order to collect the posted awards should certain symbols appear on that payline.

The payout for each machine and the coin requirements are listed on its front. It's imperative that you take a few moments to look at this information before you insert any coins. I cannot tell you how many times I have seen gamblers insert a dollar token and miss collecting on the $100 jackpot that requires $3 to win.

The most common multiple-coin machines are;

1-Way. There is only one horizontal payline, but payout increases for each additional coin played. The majority of these are two- or three-coin machines. Most of the payout increases are proportional, but the full complement of coins must be played in order to win the jackpots on some machines or the superjackpots on others. Generally, those superjackpots pay out about four times the amount that one would win with one less coin inserted, i.e., one $1 token, $200; two $1 tokens, $400; three $1 tokens, $1,600.

3-Way. There are three parallel paylines, each reading horizontally from left to right. Winning combinations on any of the lines pay out if three coins have been played.

5-Way. Three horizontal paylines and two diagonals, going from left bottom to right top and left top to right bottom. Winning combinations on any of the lines pay out if five coins have been played. The fifth-line jackpot is substantially larger than those on other lines.

Smaller jackpots are paid out automatically by the machines. Larger ones may pay a certain number of coins automatically and the balance is paid by an attendant, or the entire amount may be hand-paid. If you hit a jackpot and all of the coins are not disbursed by the machine, do not play the machine again until an attendant gives you the rest of your winnings.

Maximizing Your Money. Payouts vary from machine to machine. Identical-looking slots in the same casino may pay amounts that are different from each other on winning combinations—especially on their jackpots. Therefore, it's a smart idea to look around before you start playing. If the machines have the same number of symbols on their reels in the same combinations (and most identical machines do), you'll have a better chance on those with the higher payouts.

Some casinos advertise a 99 percent payback on certain machines, and they are required by law to tell the truth about this. What the 99 percent figure means is that over a prolonged period of time the machine pays back 99¢ on the dollar.

However, this does *not* mean that if you put $100 in a machine, you will get $99 back. Or that you'll get at least $990 back on a $1,000 investment. You might get $990 or you might get $3,000 or you might get $255.

Remember, you'll be paid for winning combinations that appear on lit lines only, so be sure that your coins register as you put them in (sometimes the receptors are not working properly and fail to accept every coin, dropping them into the tray instead).

Obviously, the greater the number of reels, the more difficult it is to line up symbols all of the same kind or in a certain sequence; hence, the higher payouts (Megabucks, Quartermania, and Nevada Nickels—the computer-linked machines throughout the state with gigantic payouts—all are four-reel machines). And generally, the more different symbols a machine has on its reels, the more difficult it is to line up the big wins, since more nonwinning combinations are possible.

Lots of slot machines have chairs attached or placed in front of them. While it may add to your comfort to sit while you play, that comfort also entices you to stay at a machine longer. If you really don't want to gamble for more than a few minutes, stand up.

Video Poker

Extremely popular, supposedly the most addictive of any of the coin machines, these computerized games can be found in just about every casino. What makes them so intriguing is their decision-making element, which is missing from slot machines.

The first machines, introduced about twenty years ago, were regular draw-poker machines. Since then, variations such as Deuces Wild, Jokers Wild, and Deuces and Jokers Wild have been added.

The basic concept of the machines is the same as that of draw poker as played in poker rooms. The object is to get the best hand possible in two tries, the deal and the draw.

In most cases, if you choose to play a 25¢ machine that returns bets on a pair of jacks or better, you will be able to play for an hour or more on a $20 investment. The length-of-time-played/money-spent ratio is much more in the player's favor than with the slots, for example, where the typical grind rate on multiple-coin nickel machines has been estimated at $25 an hour, on dime machines, about $50 an hour, and approximately $125 on quarter machines.

The first step to winning at traditional video draw poker is choosing the right kind of machine. Almost all of the machines return bets on a pair of jacks or better—which, if you play correctly, allows you to play lots of hands on a roll of coins. And the more plays you get for your money, the more chance you have of hitting winning combinations.

Payout rates vary considerably. Most likely, the best you'll see for single-coin bets on regular video poker machines with the pair of jacks or better feature are as follows:

royal flush	250 coins (five coins pays $1,000)
straight flush	50 coins
four of a kind	25 coins
full house	9 coins
flush	6 coins

straight	4 coins
three of a kind	3 coins
two pairs	2 coins

You'll be more apt to find machines that pay eight coins for a full house and five a straight. If payouts are any lower than this, keep looking—even if you have to go to another casino.

On machines that don't pay on a pair of jacks or better—and they're becoming rare—royals, three of a kind, and two pairs usually pay the same as above, but the other combinations pay slightly to decidedly more. A straight flush commonly pays 100 coins; four of a kind, 40; full house, 10; flushes, 7; and straights, 5.

Almost all the machines pay a big premium for hitting a royal flush when the maximum number of coins is played. For instance, on a five-coin quarter machine, you could win $250 on four coins played, but $1,000 if all five coins were inserted.

Before you start to play, look closely at the buttons on your machine. On most machines, square buttons placed directly under each card say HOLD. But on certain machines (they're definitely in the minority) those buttons say DISCARD. Other buttons on the machine say DEAL, DRAW (the deal/draw function is usually, but not always, performed by a single button), CANCEL, STAND, and COLLECT. These buttons are not in the same order on all makes of machines. And you can lose money if you press the wrong one.

As coins are inserted into the slot, the payback rates for the various winning combinations will appear on the video screen above the playing area, increasing proportionately with the insertion of each coin (except in the case of the royal, as mentioned above). Machines take from one to five, eight, or ten coins.

In some casinos, a group of video poker machines may be linked together, with a computerized readout above the bank of machines, with the jackpot increasing each time coins are put into any of the machines.

After the money is inserted, the player presses the DEAL button and five cards appear on the screen. The player chooses the cards he or she wishes to hold (or discard, if the machine plays that way) and presses the appropriate buttons. On some older-model machines, the CANCEL button can be used when the wrong buttons have been pushed; on later-model machines, pushing a button the second time negates the first.

When the player has made the choices, he or she presses the DRAW button, which causes the unwanted cards to disappear from the screen and others to take their places. In the case you're dealt a "natural" (a winning combination such as a royal, straight flush, four of a kind, full house, flush, or straight), press the STAND button and you'll be paid. On machines without this button, it will be necessary to press the HOLD buttons under each of the five cards. On most later-model machines, when a royal is hit with maximum coins played, the coins are automatically registered as soon as the combination is hit.

You can play from ten to fifteen games a minute, depending upon how fast the coin-receiving action and payout are on a particular machine and how long you spend deciding which cards to keep. If you play nonstop, that means six hundred to nine hundred games per hour.

According to officials of IGT, one of the leading video-poker-machine manufacturers, the inner workings of the machines use a pseudo-random-number generation, and each new game involves a deal from all fifty-two cards in the deck. If this is so, these are your chances of being dealt the various winning combinations:

pair of jacks or better	1 in 2.4
two pairs	1 in 21
three of a kind	1 in 47
straight	1 in 255
flush	1 in 509
full house	1 in 694
four of a kind	1 in 4,165

straight flush	1 in 72,193
royal flush	1 in 649,740

Despite what the company people say, experienced video poker players are convinced that these combinations come up far more often.

In Deuces Wild video poker, the four twos are wild, which makes winning combinations come up far more often than in the traditional computer game. Payouts, as a result, are less. Look for machines with these payouts on one coin:

royal flush without deuces	250 (five coins pays $1,000)
four deuces	200
royal flush with deuces	25
five of a kind	15
straight flush	9
full house	3
flush	2
straight	2
three of a kind	1

In the Joker Poker game, there's one joker added to the fifty-two-card deck, and the best payout rates look like this:

royal flush, without joker	500 (five coins pays $1,000)
five of a kind	200
royal flush, with joker	100
straight flush	50
four of a kind	20
full house	10
flush	6
straight	5
three of a kind	2
two pair	1
kings or better	1

Machines with both jokers and deuces wild offer the lowest

payouts. However, the jackpot for hitting all four deuces plus the joker with all five coins played is $4,000 on some 25¢ machines—as high as you'll find for many video poker machines that take dollar tokens.

Maximizing Your Money. The biggest clue as to where you'll find the best-paying video poker machines is to find a casino that's patronized by the locals. In Las Vegas, hundreds of residents play the game regularly—some of them, every day— and they've made it their business to find out where the loosest machines are.

Look for Jokers Wild machines that return your bet on a pair of kings and higher, or at least on a pair of aces.

To further tip the odds in your favor, here's a rundown of the mistakes typical unsuccessful players make:

1. Talking to friends while playing and taking their advice— no matter how bad it may be. This is okay if your object is having a good time without caring whether you win or not. But to maximize profits, you really have to pay attention to what you're doing in this game.

2. Playing hunches: holding a single low card just because it's your lucky number, rather than hanging on to a face card, which, if paired, will give you another shot at a bigger payout.

3. Bucking the odds: holding three nonconsecutive low cards of the same suit instead of two kings, drawing to an inside straight when you could hold a pair, taking the big chance consistently rather than settling for a smaller payback on a sure thing.

4. Playing when you're tired. If you're not alert, you'll make mistakes, and there's nothing worse than accidentally pressing the DRAW button rather than standing when the machine has cooperated by dealing you four of a kind.

21 (Blackjack)

Two cards are dealt facedown to each player by the dealer. The dealer's first card faces up; the second, down. The object of the game is to hold cards that total twenty-one or to come closer to twenty-one than the cards held by the dealer. The king, queen, and jack each count ten. The cards from two to ten are counted at their face value. An ace can be counted either as one or eleven. An ace with any king, queen, jack, or ten is called a blackjack. If you're dealt this combination, turn your cards faceup immediately and the dealer will pay you one and a half times your bet, unless the dealer also has a blackjack. In this case, no money or chips change hands. When the dealer's and player's cards total the same amount, it's called a push.

If you aren't dealt a blackjack, you may want the dealer to "hit" you (deal you another card or more). You may be dealt as many cards as you want, one at a time, so long as your cards don't total more than twenty-one. If the total goes over twenty-one, you go "bust" and lose. In this case, you turn your cards faceup. When you do not want to be hit, you may "stand" by sliding your cards facedown under your bet.

After all the players at a table have their cards either in a stand position, have been dealt a blackjack, or have gone bust, the dealer turns his or her down card faceup and stands or draws more cards as necessary. The dealer must draw to any count up to and including sixteen and stand on seventeen, except a "soft" seventeen (any combination of cards containing an ace, but not a ten, that totals seventeen). When the dealer has a soft seventeen, the dealer must draw.

Craps

Granted, the craps table layout looks pretty complicated. But in reality, it's a fairly simple game. In each game, one of the players is the "shooter." The shooter throws a pair of dice in what is called the "come-out-roll." On that roll, when the shooter rolls a seven or eleven, he (and the bettors who bet with the shooter) win. If the shooter rolls craps (a two, three, or twelve), the shooter and those who bet with him or her lose.

When any of the other totals (four, five, six, eight, nine, or ten) come up, that number becomes the established point, and the shooter has to continue rolling the dice until he makes that number again in order to win. However, if the shooter rolls a seven before he makes his point, he "sevens-out" and loses. The next shooter to the left then throws the dice.

The bets you can make follow:

Pass line—This is what you play if you're betting with the shooter—that he will roll a seven or eleven on the come-out roll; that he won't roll a two, three, or twelve. When the point is established—remember, that's a four, five, six, eight, nine, or ten—the shooter must roll it again before he throws a seven.

Don't pass—You're betting against the shooter on this one, so you'll win if he or she rolls two, three, or twelve on the come-out. You'll lose if the shooter throws a seven or eleven, or if the shooter rolls the established point before rolling a seven. As you can see, this bet is the exact opposite of the pass. You are limited to one pass/don't-pass bet per roll.

Come—The same as the pass bet, except that it can only be placed after a point is established.

Don't come—The same as the don't-pass bet, except that it can only be placed after a point is established. You can place as many consecutive come/don't-come bets as you like.

Place—A bet on any or all of the following: four, five, six, eight, nine, ten (place numbers). It says that the numbers betted on will be thrown before a seven.

The field—A one-roll bet that a two, three, four, nine, ten, eleven, or twelve will be rolled. If a five, six, seven, or eight is rolled, the bet is lost.

Big six and big eight—You can make this bet on either or both of these numbers at any time. You win if the number(s) you choose is rolled before a seven is thrown.

Hard way—This bet says that the number you have chosen (it must be an even number) will be made by rolling the dice so that the same number is up on each, e.g., two sixes for a twelve.

There are still other bets you can make, but it's a good idea to stick to the basics until you have had a fair amount of hands-on experience. Even then, you may decide to limit your wagering to come and pass bets, since they give you a much better chance of winning than the others.

Maximizing Your Money.   Sometimes when you're playing, you may be "on a roll." The mistake is to think that roll will last for three hours more. When you get a reasonable amount ahead, be prepared to cash in your chips as soon as your luck starts turning.

If you play craps primarily because you like the excitement that goes with each toss of the dice, you'll be happy to know there are still some 25¢ games in Las Vegas. Slots-A-Fun is one casino where you'll find them.

Keno

To play, mark from one to fifteen of the eighty numbers on a keno ticket. You'll find these tickets in areas with counters and desklike seats called keno lounges. The next step is to take your ticket to the counter and give it to a keno writer, who will copy the ticket and write the amount of your bet in the margin. In most Las Vegas casinos, the minimum amount you can bet is one or two dollars.

Each game is assigned a number in sequence, and tickets must be purchased prior to the time the game is closed. During the course of the game, eighty Ping-Pong-type balls, numbered from one to eighty, are mechanically agitated in a plastic or wire container. One by one, twenty of these balls are ejected and their numbers are illuminated on keno flashboards throughout the casino.

Whether you win or not depends upon how many of the numbers marked on your ticket light up on the keno board. Also, your ticket number must correspond to the game number on the lighted board. If you play a five-spot ticket (five numbers marked), for example, at least three of those numbers must come up. On a ten-spot ticket, you must "catch" at least five.

A variation, called the Way Ticket, allows playing two or more combinations of numbers on a single ticket. Diagrammed explanations of how Way Tickets work are available in most keno lounges.

Another keno variation is called 20/40 keno. After the first twenty balls are mechanically expelled, twenty more are ejected. Players who buy forty-ball cards are paid when a certain number of their numbers are caught (or conversely, when none—or only a specified low number of them—come up.)

If you want to play keno while eating in a casino restaurant or having a drink at the bar, keno runners will take your tickets and money to the counters for you—and bring you your winnings (be sure to tip when you win).

Maximizing Your Money. The house edge in keno is the highest of any of the games. This would make it one of the least attractive except for the fact that is also the slowest game, so your money disappears at about the same per-hour rate.

The eight-spot is one of the most popular tickets to play since it pays the highest jackpot for the least number of correct selections—$50,000 when all eight numbers are caught. But you will find that when you catch four of your numbers, you only get your money back, and catching half the numbers when the odds are one in four is a feat in itself.

Before you decide to play keno for money, play twenty or more "make-believe" games. Fill out the tickets, but don't bring them to the ticket counter. Then, after each game, write down the money you would have spent and the money you would have won. The odds are very good that you'll be happy you didn't play for cash.

After all this, if you *must* play a game, check over all your used tickets to see if any numbers came up an abnormally large percentage of the time. Then mark a card with those numbers only (there probably won't be more than two or three of them if there are any) on the chance that there's something about the composition of certain of the numbered balls that's causing them to be ejected more often than the others. If that doesn't work—

and even if it does—play your "favorite" numbers a couple of times, then find some other game to play. In most cases, you will have spent a couple of hours with far less of a loss than you would have if you had been playing all those games for real.

Poker

The two poker games most commonly played in Las Vegas casino card rooms are seven-card stud and Texas hold 'em. Red Dog is popular, too. If you don't play poker regularly, don't even think about playing in Las Vegas. These are the big boys. Many of them make their living gambling. Play can be very fast, and there's no place for the novice or for anyone who can't afford to lose a lot of money in a very short time.

Maximizing Your Money. Four variations on poker are played at casino tables (rather than in the poker room) that you can play for generally lower stakes and that don't move as fast. Three of the games—sic bo, fan-tan, and pai gow—have Chinese origins. The fourth, Caribbean stud, is a newcomer that is fast becoming popular.

Sic bo is an ancient oriental game centering around three dice in a seated shaker. About fifty possible bets can be placed on the table layout. They include the various numbers that all three dice will total when tossed, and the combinations of numbers that can occur.

Fan-tan players place their bets on a square board with numbered sides (one, two, three, and four) or on areas at the corners between the numbers. When all bets are placed, the dealer removes a portion of a pile of beans that is concealed by a brass bowl. When the beans are exposed, the dealer divides the beans with a thin wand into rows of four until only four, three, two, or one bean(s) remain. The number of beans remaining determines which are the winning numbers.

Pai gow is a complicated game played with thirty-two specially designed dominoes, and errors in playing result in disqualification, so the game is patronized mostly by Orientals who have played it for years. *Pai gow poker,* however, is a table game that's become popular with Orientals and Occidentals alike. A combination of pai gow and poker, it is played with an ordinary deck of fifty-two cards plus one joker. The joker is used as an ace or to complete a straight flush.

Players are dealt seven cards each, which are then arranged into two hands. One hand contains five cards and is called the high hand. The second hand with two cards is known as the low hand. The object of the game is to win the bet by having both the high and low hands rank higher than the respective hands of the banker. The ranking is determined by traditional poker rules. If both hands rank lower, the wager is lost to the banker. If either hand wins while the other loses, the wager is a "push" and no money changes hands. The house handles all bets and charges a five percent commission on all winning wagers.

Caribbean stud is a beat-the-dealer game played at a table much like those on which 21 is played. Players receive five cards facedown and the dealer receives four cards facedown and one card up after bets have been placed by each player in his or her "ante box."

To participate in the progressive jackpot (a payout to players who have any of the winning poker combinations such as three of a kind or a full house), players must drop dollar tokens into the slots in front of their ante boxes.

If a player thinks his hand cannot beat the dealer's hand, he folds and loses his ante bet. If he thinks his hand will beat the dealer's hand, he must place a bet of exactly twice the amount of the ante bet to call the dealer.

The dealer must have an ace/king or higher to continue. If the dealer cannot open with at least ace/king, the hand is over. The dealer collects the cards and pays even money on all the ante bets of players who did not fold.

If the dealer's hand is high enough to open, and the player's hand is higher, the player will be paid even money on the ante bet and a bonus amount on the call bet, ranging from two to one to a hundred to one.

And There are More

Computerized 21 Machines

After inserting coins (usually 25¢ or $1 tokens), the player presses the DEAL button. Two dealer cards appear at the top of the screen, one faceup and the other facedown. Below are the player's two cards, both faceup. If the dealer's two cards total twenty-one, the second card flips faceup and the game is over with the player losing (some 21 machines return the coins in case of a tie). If the dealer's cards total less than twenty-one, the player has the option of pressing the HIT button for an additional card or cards. If the total reaches more than twenty-one, the game is over and the player loses. When the player is satisfied with a hand, he or she presses the STAND button, at which time the dealer's hidden card is exposed. If the dealer has seventeen or more points, he must stand. Otherwise, additional cards are dealt. If the player's total is closer to twenty-one than the dealer's, the player receives double his or her money from the machine. Just play this one as you would if you were in a game with a live dealer.

Computerized Keno

The player inserts a coin, presses the ERASE button, then with a pointer attached to the left front of the machine "marks" the eighty-number playing board on the screen with the numbers he or she wishes to play. One to ten numbers can be marked on most machines. As the numbers are marked, the number of catches required to win appears with its respective payout on an upper screen. As soon as the PLAY button is pressed, twenty numbers are illuminated in rapid succession on the playing board. As each of the player's numbers is "caught," it's indicated by a check mark.

Maximizing Your Money. This is another game that's extremely hypnotic. Play takes only seconds, and most machines can gobble up to five coins per game. Since the odds are heavily weighted in favor of the house, those quarters can go very fast, and it's possible to lose more than $50 in quarters in a half hour.

Roulette

The roulette wheel has thirty-six numbers from 1 to 36 marked on it, plus a 0 and 00. The numbers are alternately colored red and black, but the 0 and 00 are green. When the players have placed most of their bets by putting their chips on the layout containing all the numbers plus combinations of numbers and odd/even number options, the dealer spins a small white ball in the opposite direction of the spinning wheel. Bets may be placed until the ball is ready to leave the track and the dealer signals that betting is closed. The number above which the ball stops is the winner. Single-number wins, including 0 and 00, usually pay around thirty-five to one. Odds vary with the combination bets.

Maximizing Your Money. Stay away from this one. The house advantage is around 5.25 percent—too high to make the game attractive to anyone wanting to stretch their casino dollars.

PM Wheel

The pari-mutuel wheel, sometimes called the wheel of fortune or big six, is a wheel of about a six-foot diameter. Bets are placed on a layout that corresponds to the money denominations displayed in various positions on the wheel. When all the bets are in, the dealer spins the wheel and the money winners are those who have bet on the denominations where the pointer comes to rest. On most PM wheels, a bet on the $20 bill pays twenty to one; $10 pays ten to one; $5 pays five to one; $2 pays two to one, and $1 pays even money.

Maximizing Your Money. Resist temptation on this one, too.

Baccarat (pronounced "bak*arah*").

The Americanized version of chemin de fer, this game is played with eight decks of cards, shuffled by the croupier and dealt from a box called the shoe. Two hands of two or three cards each—called the "player's" and the "banker's"—are dealt. Bettors can wager on either hand or on a tie. "Bank" bettors must pay the house a commission (usually 5 percent, but occasionally lower) on winning bets.

The object of the game is to come as close as possible to nine points. All cards from ace through ten are counted at face value. Each face card has a value of ten. The cards in each hand are totaled, but only the last digit is used. For example, ten plus six equals sixteen (scored as six). Nine plus five plus ten equals twenty-four (scored as four). Whether two or three cards are dealt to a hand depends on the following:

When player's hand holds two cards totaling

0 1 2 3 4 5	must draw third card
6 7	must stand
8 9	a natural; bank cannot draw

When banker's hand holds two cards totaling

3	draws third card except when player's third card is 8
4	draws third card when player's third card is 2 through 7
5	draws third card when player's third card is 4, 5, 6, or 7
6	draws third card when player's third card is 6 or 7
7	must stand
8 or 9	a natural; player cannot draw

Maximizing Your Money. This is a game that's enjoyable if you know the rules well enough to relax. If you don't, it's more fun than most casino games to watch. Above all, don't bet on ties—the house has a 14 percent edge on tie bets.

Bingo

Las Vegas has several *huge* bingo parlors. The largest of them— at the Showboat Hotel/Casino and the Triple J Bingo Hall & Casino in nearby Henderson—each accommodates fifteen hundred people. You'll find other big bingo games in casinos including Aladdin, Arizona Charlie's, Frontier, Gold Coast, Harrah's, Palace Station, and Santa Fe.

Although the rules vary slightly at the different establishments, essentially the same variations of the game are played. Pressurized blowers mix the numbered balls and force them into a position to be racked one at a time so that they are in view of the players. The numbers are called out over the public-address system and also appear on lighted bingo boards.

Each bingo card has five vertical rows of five numbers each under the letters *B, I, G,* and *O,* and four numbers plus a free space under N. When a number that is on a player's card is called, the player covers it by moving a shutter from left to right so that number is covered or marks the number with a dauber (sort of like a supersize felt pen).

Regular bingo, with the object of getting any five numbers in a row—horizontally, vertically, diagonally—before the other players, is the game most often played. Cover-all bingo requires all twenty-four numbers on the board to be covered by the time a specified amount of numbers have been called. In many bingo parlors, that amount is increased (often along with the size of the cash prize) with each cover-all game until the prize is won.

Other variations include four-corner bingo, in which the numbers on each of the four outside corners must be covered; big picture frame, won by being the first to cover all the numbers around the perimeter of the card; little picture frame, covering the eight numbers surrounding the free space; big X, covering letters on both diagonals to form an *X*, and forming such letters at *T, H, C, L, Z,* and *E.*

At most casino bingo parlors, you buy cards before the session begins that are good for all the games played during a certain time period (usually ten games played in about an hour to an hour and fifteen minutes). Minimum card prices range from $3 to about $12 for a session.

Maximizing Your Money. If you love to play bingo, you'll want to try a session, but you may not want to play any more than that. Las Vegas bingo isn't like the Friday-night games at the Elks or in the Sacred Heart parish hall back home. The cash prizes may be bigger, but hundreds of people are playing for them.

The games move quickly, and many of the players are locals who play daily—often with multiple cards at a time. If you're a novice, play the minimum number of cards. Otherwise, you may miss some of the numbers.

Most Las Vegas bingo halls are also noisy in between games, and unless there's a totally separate nonsmoking section, the atmosphere can be dreadful for people who don't want to inhale secondhand smoke. Bingo, however, can be one of the least expensive forms of gambling per hour if you spend the minimum amount on your cards.

Sports Betting

Sports books are the areas set apart from the rest of the casino, with rows of chairs and lots of giant TV screens. Each of them also has a long counter, where you can place bets on everything from the Super Bowl and major boxing matches to horse races at parks around the country.

Sports wagers are made in increments of $11. If you win, you'll get the amount of your original bet back, plus $10 for each $11 increment you bet. This gives the casino a 4.5 percent advantage, but at times casinos run promotions that allow you to bet less than the standard price and reduce the house's advantage.

Maximizing Your Money. Don't bet big on horse races as the sports books have a tremendous advantage. Whatever you like to bet on, keep an eye out for promotions that give you a better return if you win.

Place minimum bets and you'll have some good entertainment watching the games and joining in on the excitement with little cost per hour if you lose. The beer, hot dogs, and other sports-books food give the place a kind of carnival atmosphere that's fun, and the screens in the best sports books give you a far better look at the sporting event than if you were there.

Tips on Tipping

When you're offered a free drink in a casino, by all means tip—that's how the cocktail waitresses earn most of their money. If you win a sizable jackpot—especially one that requires a hand pay—hand the tip to the person who pays you the money or the change person who sold you the coins. Tips to dealers are customarily given in the form of bets placed for them, but some players give them chips, which the dealers rap once on the table to signify that they're tips and then deposit in a place that's for that purpose.

Cashing In

When you've had enough gambling for one session and have quit while you still have some coins or chips, go to a casino cage or the cashier's counter to cash them in.

If you're lucky enough to hit a big jackpot, you'll be asked to show identification with your social security number before you can collect.

Big jackpots attract lots of attention—not always from people with honorable intentions. So ask that your winnings be in the form of a check. Then mail it in an envelope to your bank

Do-it-yourself Gambling Junkets

You can keep your gambling expenses to a minimum—even maybe turn a profit—and get lots of exercise into the bargain by using the gaming-table coupons you have collected. Here's how.

Map at the ready, organize your coupons in order of the casinos you'll come to as you walk along the Strip (or downtown). Which part of the Strip you choose should be determined in part by the value of the various coupons in your stash.

For example, Slots-A-Fun and Silver City are close to each other. Both of them have easily obtained funbooks that contain two-for-one coupons. This means you bet a dollar, and if you win, get two dollars back in addition to your original bet—a far better deal than coupons that pay $7 when you win a $5 bet. First, you invest less money with each bet, and in addition, your rate of return is far better.

Before you set out, determine how much your gambling stake will be—$10, $20, $30—and grab any coupons for free slot pulls, drinks, or other refreshments at the casinos where you plan to use your table-play coupons.

Go to the first casino on your route, play the coupons for games you enjoy, pocket any winnings, and hike to the next casino. If you've collected several funbooks from the same casino, better go to different tables to use your coupons, since the coupons might have words like "one per person per visit" printed on them.

You can expect to win almost as often as you lose at blackjack, and also at craps, if you make only come and

> pass bets. That means you have a good chance of coming out a few dollars ahead if you gamble only when you have coupons to put down with your bets. And chances are, your losses will be minimal. If you play twenty two-to-one coupons in the course of your gambling junket, you need only to win seven times to come out about even.

or home (you can get an envelope and buy a stamp at the hotel desk or gift shop). If you're paid in cash and the amount is sizable, ask to have someone escort you to your hotel room or the nearest place where you can get a cashier's check made out to yourself.

Gambler's Fatigue

It's hard work gambling, and if you spend more than a couple of hours sitting at a 21 table or playing the slots, you're bound to feel twinges in your posterior, as well as in your upper back and shoulders.

Take a break every once in a while, since tired and sore players make mistakes—not to mention feeling stiff the next day. The best time to take a break is when you're having a streak of bad luck, as it gives you time to restore your gambling sanity, especially if you go outside or into a nongaming area of the building. Never forget that the flashing lights, the music, the hypnotic sounds—even the colors—have been scientifically calculated to make people play the games. There's even talk of yet another device—an aroma sprayed in the air that intensifies the gambler's feeling of well-being.

Gambling Tourneys

Although the Amarillo Slim and World Series of Poker tournaments had been going on for more than a decade, competitions featuring other casino games such as 21, keno, slots, and video poker didn't become popular until the mid-eighties. Now, most major casinos in Las Vegas put on several weekend tournaments during the year, and many of them hold daily tournaments as well.

The entry fee varies with each weekend tournament and usually pays for a complete tournament package, attractively merchandised in glossy brochures. Although the fees often run $1,000 or higher, those that include include hotel lodging for one to three nights as well as meals and drinks for the participant and guest can run as low as $300.

Tourney weekends usually offer a series of parties based on a central theme—Valentine's Day, Reeling in Paradise, Winter Splendor—in addition to tournament play. The first night may feature a cocktail party, or it might be a hoedown or a sock hop. Traditionally, tournaments end with an awards brunch or dinner. In between rounds of play, participants socialize with friends they've met at previous tournaments, and more likely than not, they gamble.

Tournament play is either of the "buy-in" or "no buy-ins" variety. In the former category, players may pay additional money as a tournament progresses in order to buy more chips or plays on a machine. This type of competition can be extremely expensive as players get carried away with their desire to win.

When no buy-ins are allowed, poker, dice, and blackjack tournament participants are given a certain number of chips at the beginning of each session of play. Keno tournament participants get a specific amount of scrip that can be exchanged for keno tickets. The number of points, chips, or winning numbers accumulated determines the winners. This kind of tournament guarantees a player that expenditures will be limited to the money paid at the outset of play.

Meters or points tabulated by attendants are used in most slot tourneys, rather than slot machine tokens. Most tournament rules stipulate that the player who has accumulated the most points at the end of a specified period of time is the winner, and all players stay in the competition for the entire session.

Since entry fees at the weekend tournaments are steep, they're usually not a bargain except for about the 20 percent of the participants who win the top prizes. In a tournament with an entry fee of $1,000 and 350 participants, the awards will look something like this:

1st place	.$100,000
2nd place	.35,000
3rd place	.25,000
4th place	.15,000
5th place	.10,000
6th place	.8,000
7th place	.7,000
8th place	.6,000
9th place	.5,000
10th place	.4,000
11–20th place (each)	.1,100
21st–50th place (each)	.950
51st–100th place (each)	.550
101st–150th place (each)	.300
151st–200th place (each)	.250
20 session winners (each)	.500

Daily tournaments, by contrast, can be great bargains—when they're free. Most of them are slot contests; the others almost always 21 or video poker. Though an increasing number of daily tourneys now require entry fees ranging from $10 to $25, you'll still be able to find those that cost absolutely nothing. Though hundreds of people may enter, you still have the excitement of playing with the hope of winning a prize.

Almost all of the daily 21 tournaments start participants off with a certain number of chips, and the players who amass the highest monetary value based on the chips they have at the and of the game advance to the semifinal and final rounds. Daily slot and video poker tournaments are played on metered machines, with the players accumulating the highest number of points winning their rounds.

Good luck!

14

♠

Postscript

Nevada, since its first permanent settlement in 1851, has ridden on a roller coaster of boom or bust; bonanza or borrasco.

And following true to historical form, Las Vegas is the Boomtown USA of the 1990s. Always unique among the world's tourist attractions, Nevada's largest city set about during the past decade to reinvent itself. No longer just a downtown cluster and three-mile strip of glitz and dazzle, it has become a mother lode of megaresorts that potential gambling competition in any other part of the country would be daunted to duplicate. It also became one of the fastest growing cities in the nation.

The trend shows no signs of abating. Every source agrees that the Las Vegas population figure of one million is correct, and new residents continue moving into the houses and condos in dozens of developments under construction. Some projections show that in the next century, Las Vegas may well be one of the largest cities in the U.S. The estimated 1996 tourist count, which ranges from 30 to 36 million, is expected to keep rising as well.

In the city where telephone directories are published every six months to keep pace, shopping centers, restaurants, nightclubs, hotel/casinos, chain stores, and individual businesses open, go belly up, move, expand, change names, and change owners with regularity. To add to the confusion, the telephone company has had to institute new exchanges to accommodate the growing demand for lines, so that many numbers that two years ago had one three-digit prefix, now have another.

We have updated the preceding chapters to reflect these changes. But so many new facilities and attractions have come on line since this book first came out in 1995, that an entire new chapter is necessary to tell you about them.

What's New

Most dazzling of the city's attractions has to be the Fremont Street Experience, which premiered in December 1995. From Main Street to Fourth Street, the principal stretch of Glitter Gulch downtown has been transformed into a pedestrian mall and covered with a 90-foot-high space frame. Set into the frame's surface are 2.1 million lights, and the columns that hold up the frame contain 40 speakers.

Each night, the lights come to life in multi-sensory shows presented on the hour from 6 to 11 P.M., with sound from the speakers accompanying the movements of the images, whether they be cowboys in a shootout, high-kicking cancan girls or coyotes howling at the moon.

If you're sensitive to noise, you might want to bring along earplugs, but even so you can't help but marvel at the intricacy of the computer-generated displays overhead. Other free entertainment, from musical productions and sporting events to holiday festivities, is held beneath the canopy through the year.

The Hard Rock Hotel (4475 Paradise Road; 702-693-5000), is touted as the "world's first rock-and-roll hotel and casino." Decorated with rock and roll memorabilia and supersize guitar logo, the 11-story hotel is within easy walking distance of the Strip and features a 1,200-seat theater called The Joint, where rock concerts are the main attraction.

Among the special events held at the Hard Rock in 1996 was the fifth annual Miller Lite King of the Beach volleyball tournament, for which a sandy beach surrounded by 4,500-seat bleachers was constructed in the parking lot. By the way, the hotel/casino advertises philanthropic slot machines that "bene-fit the Save the Rain Forest Foundation."

Two "neighborhood" casinos, Texas (2101 Texas Star Lane; 702-631-1000) and Fiesta (2400 N. Rancho Drive; 702-631-7000) have joined the Santa Fe in Northwest Las Vegas. Located near retirement communities, these casinos are already popular with the locals and tourists who prefer the friendliness of smaller gambling places.

The southwest-themed Fiesta gives away a number of worth-while freebies—among them a hotdog, frozen yogurt cone, and a free breakfast, lunch, or dinner buffet. Inside the Texas, where interior walls are recreations of the facades of early-day buildings of the Lone Star State, you'll discover some terrific $1.99 breakfast specials that will keep you full until dinner.

Sci-fi fans and other forward-looking types will want to check out Virtual World (30523 Las Vegas Boulevard S.; 702-369-3583), which its brochures describe as "The World's First Location-Based Virtual Reality Center."

At the digital theme park, you receive one-on-one instruc-tion on how to navigate in the virtual reality environment of your choice. Then, in a "relocation pod" at the controls of your interdimensional vehicle, you and the other pilots in your mission are dropped into your chosen dimension where you are free to move and interact at will. Two adventures are currently available. One involves piloting a two-legged tank in a 31st Century war and the other, racing through the canals of Mars. The cost per mission is $7 Monday–Friday before 5 P.M.; $8, Monday–Thursday after 5 P.M. and $9, Friday after 5 P.M., all day Saturday, Sunday, and holidays.

Out of this world in another way is a one-of-its-kind spectacular called Stratosphere (2000 Las Vegas Boulevard S.; 702-383-4752). The name refers to the new megaresort's tower that soars 1,149 feet in the air—equivalent in height to a 100-story building. The resort includes 1,500 guest rooms and suites, 97,000 square feet of casino space, restaurants and bars.

The tower, however, is the feature that most people will

want to see—for several reasons. First of all, it contains High Roller, the world's highest roller coaster, which starts at more than 900 feet above the ground. Then there's Space Shot, a state-of-the-art thrill ride that shoots riders 160 feet straight up. Indoor and outdoor observation decks, a 360-seat revolving restaurant and 200-seat cocktail lounge plus three wedding chapels are also a part of the gigantic skyrise.

A King Kong amusement, guaranteed to raise goosebumps, is the tower's newest attraction. The mechanical beast (with 48 passengers in his belly) climbs 600 feet up the tower, growls, moves his head and arms, fights off attacking airplanes, then free-falls 30 feet. Although you have to pay for each of the tower's pleasures, they're extraordinary—to say the least.

New York-New York, with a facade composed of twelve 48-story towers re-creating the Manhattan skyline, brings a bite of the Big Apple to the Strip. The 2,035-room hotel/casino at the corner of Tropicana and Las Vegas Boulevard S. (1-800-693-6763) carries out its New York theme with replicas of the Empire State building, Central Park, the Statue of Liberty and other famous landmarks, including the Brooklyn Bridge walkway entrance.

Along with restaurants, bars, a casino, and theater, New York-New York also features an entertainment center with rides such as a Coney Island-style roller coaster. Although you would imagine the amusement center to be in competition with the MGM Grand theme park across the street, MGM is one of the two principals in the New York-New York operation—an example of the current trend for owners of existing hotel/casinos to co-venture construction of new properties.

Another new joint venture hotel/casino is Monte Carlo (Flamingo Road and Las Vegas Boulevard S.; 702-794-3881), with the Mirage Group and Circus/Circus as 50-50 partners. The complex, themed to evoke images of the Place du Casino in Monaco's Monte Carlo at the turn of the century, the complex incorporates fanciful arches, chandeliered domes, ornate fountains and gas-lit promenades into its design.

Advertising "the experience of royalty for a value price," the hotel/casino is targeting the mass-market player and tourist. Along with the hotel's traditional restaurants, there's a food court, with Haagen Dazs, McDonald's and Nathan's among the concessions. A full-service health spa, with a 2,000-square-foot exercise room and tennis courts are available to guests eager to burn off the calories.

Orleans (4500 W. Tropicana Avenue; 800-331-5334), with lacy wrought iron balconies, New Orleans jazz and a 40-foot atrium highlighted by lush landscaping, is an 840-room hotel/casino west of the Strip. In addition to a large casino area, the property's features include a wedding chapel, restaurants, convention space, and a Mardi Gras bar, with masks and other Carnival memorabilia providing the decoration. There's also a bayou-themed Crawfish Bar, a 70-lane bowling center and a free child care operation.

During the past months, other major properties have expanded in a big way. For instance, Luxor spent some $240 million to build a tower with 1,970 guest rooms, a 1,500-seat showroom, a spa and convention space. Circus-Circus built a 1,200-room tower and Boardwalk/Holiday Inn added a 456-room tower, a parking garage, buffet, casino, and convention space.

Race car afficionados are talking about the remake of the Las Vegas Motor Speedway into a 107,000-seat facility. The first completely new super speedway to be built in the Southwest in more than twenty years, it was site of the 1996 NASCAR Super-Truck series finale. The $100 million, 1,500-acre facility includes 24 different race tracks, food courts, two viewing levels for motorhome owners, three levels of open air grandstand seating, and luxury skybox suites. All this, plus an only-in-Las Vegas-feature—a wedding chapel where the stained glass windows have a racing motif. The raceway is located at 7000 Las Vegas Boulevard N. (702-644-4444).

The new Hoover Dam Visitor Center is something to write home about, too. With two theaters, an exhibit gallery, and an overlook where you can get an awesome view of the gigantic dam, it's the place where walking tours of the facility begin (see chapter 8). There's also a film, "The Building of Hoover Dam," that you shouldn't miss.

Other new Las Vegas attractions include Barley's, the world's only microbrewery/casino (4300 East Sunset Road; 702-458-2739) where a 40-foot grain silo provides unusual entrance decor. Three specialty beers—Blue Diamond, Red Rock and Black Mountain—all named for southern Nevada landmarks—are brewed on the premises behind a glass wall in full view of casino customers.

There's something new for the small fry, too. Kids Quest at Boulder Station (4111 Boulder Highway; 702-432-7777) and Stratosphere is a franchise operation which consists of activity centers certain to keep children busy while parents go off on their own.

Included in the recreational lineup are big-screen video, interactive CD-Rom stations, Barbie Land, Kids Karaoke, and play structures with tunnels, tubes, and slides. Kids Quest facilities also have special rooms for six-week to 30-month-old children. Charges at the Boulder Station operation are $5 per hour per child with a three and a half hour maximum. The facility is open daily 9 A.M.–11 P.M. (midnight on Friday and Saturday). At Stratosphere, prices and hours are comparable. If you check with sitter prices in chapter 10, you'll find that Kids Quest is less expensive, with lots of child appeal in the bargain.

On the shopping scene, a 28-foot gilded statue of the priest Xuanzang and his three disciples—an irreverent monkey, a greedy but loveable boar and a hard-working river goblin—stands in front of the new Chinatown Plaza (4215 Spring Mountain Road; 702-221-8448). Even though the shopping center has traditional Chinese golden tile roofs, inside is a contemporary two-story complex of stores, offices, and restaurants.

Marco Polo Furniture features elegant handcrafted Chinese furniture in rosewood, cherry, and bamboo. An oriental foods store and a bakery (see chapter 4) as well as other businesses cater primarily to Las Vegas's Oriental community. Restaurants include Plum Tree Inn with Mandarin cuisine, Shanghai Restaurant, China Express, Sam Woo Bar-B-Q, Pho Vietnam Restaurant and Kim Tai Seafood. In addition to interesting shopping and dining, there's often free entertainment at the Chinatown Plaza. Annual Chinese New Year's celebrations and events such as a recent jade show take place in the Plaza's mall area.

Another new shopping center, Galleria, is located at Sunset Road at Stephanie Street in Henderson, on Las Vegas's southeast boundary. Decorated in a Southwest theme, highlighted by windows etched with horses, sunsets, and the like, the shopping mall will be the largest in Nevada when all construction phases are completed. Along with three waterfalls, another interesting design feature is a food court patterned after a chess board, with topiaries cut in the shape of chess pieces.

Works in Progress

But that ain't all, folks. Just when you think Las Vegas has unveiled the ultimate in glitz, gigantic dimensions, or the downright bizarre, shovels start breaking ground for yet other extravaganzas.

For example, a Texas-based group of more than 40 investors called Polyphase Corporation broke ground in August, 1996, for a $530 million, 110,000-seat domed stadium in downtown Las Vegas. Located southeast of the US-95 and Interstate 15 interchange, the 184-acre stadium site will also contain shops, restaurants and a non-gaming hotel. The group aims to bring major league baseball to Las Vegas and also has Superbowl dreams.

Bellagio (Flamingo Road and Las Vegas Boulevard S.), which promises to be the most opulent of the properties hotel/casino magnate Steve Wynn has produced so far, gets its inspiration from the picturesque village of the same name on the shores of Italy's Lake Como.

In lieu of a lake, the Las Vegas version features a 15-acre bay filled with treated ground water and recycled water from showers and sinks. Gardens and architecture reflect the northern Italian theme. Scheduled to open in 1997, Bellagio is, according to Wynn, "the most romantic hotel ever built in the history of the world."

Completion of the Forum Shops Phase II expansion early in 1997 will add 37 new stores, including FAO Schwartz, Fendi, Polo and Virgin Records Megastore. Among the restaurants will be Wolfgang Puck's Asian Cafe. Centerpiece of the expansion project will be the Roman Great Hall, a space 160 feet in diameter and 85 feet high, where an entertainment spectacular called Atlantis will be presented. Motif for the new portion of the Forum Shops will be similar to the romanticized Roman fantasy theme of the existing complex, with piazzas, ornate fountains and statuary.

Target year for "Star Trek: The Experience" is also 1997. Each person who visits the attraction located in the north tower of the Las Vegas Hilton will assume the identity of a Starfleet or alien crew member while participating in the imaginative world of Star Trek. Simulated rides utilizing special viewer perspective images and interactive video as well as virtual reality stations will be part of each adventure. Despite the admission price, Trekkies won't want to miss this one.

I realize that some of the places and pleasures we've mentioned in this chapter are pricey—at least by Las Vegas standards. Most of the hotels have free attractions or giveaways calculated to get people inside their moneymakers, the casinos. And even if they don't, it doesn't cost anything to walk around and gawk. To most of us, giggling at talking statues and oohing over extravagant landscaping and special effects constitutes great free entertainment.

Keep in mind, too, that in periods of growth on a scale such as Las Vegas is experiencing, there have to be times when supply exceeds demand. And that means bargains—even at the most expensive places to stay. Be on the lookout and you're sure to find them.

On the Drawing Board

Las Vegas, in truth, attracts all kinds of gamblers—not only the green-eyeshade types that sit in poker rooms or the professional sports book handicappers. Even though they come equipped with business suits and briefcases, the other forms of gamblers have tallied up the odds and are betting that their project, whether it be megaresort, domed stadium, clothing boutique or hot dog franchise—will return progressively larger jackpots to the investors as years go by.

However, the bottom line is that many of even the best-laid plans stop short of reality. Economic conditions change and money becomes tight, bids come in high, funding sources dry up, projects become unfeasible, local government and gaming permits are denied (Nevada is extremely strict in checking potential casino principals' backgrounds). Therefore, it is with a "don't count on it" caveat that we tell you about some of the plans that have been announced.

According to reliable sources, the Las Vegas Convention Authority is exploring the feasibility of building a monorail along the Strip. Talk is that they're closely monitoring the performance of the monorail that goes between Bally's and MGM Grand to determine whether the project would be worth the cost.

The backers of Paris Resort Casino, a 2,500-room resort which will be set on 25 acres adjacent to Bally's, have some rather ambitious plans, too. According to advance publicity, the resort will "Re-create the city of Paris with replicas of the Arc de Triomphe, Champs-Elysées, the Paris Opera House, Parc Monceau, the River Seine and a 50-story scale replica of the Eiffel Tower." Wow!

Officials from the Las Vegas Convention and Visitors Authority and the adjacent city of Henderson are actively pursuing the possibility of two major league baseball teams relocating their spring training camps to Southern Nevada.

A planned complex at Henderson would include a 2,500-seat

"B" squad stadium, 12 playing fields, a training facility and parking lot. "All games would be played at 9,372-seat Cashman Field, in Las Vegas, home of the Stars, Triple A farm club of the San Diego Padres.

The following dreams are also in the planning stages:

◆   The downtown Horseshoe Club's $70 million, 36-story tower and special events center

◆   Harrah's 35-story, 694-room tower, casino space and additional restaurants

◆   Fitzgerald's $14 million tower

◆   Construction of Sunset Station casino on Boulder Highway

◆   Dynasty, a 1,000-room hotel/casino across the strip from the Aladdin

◆   A 6,000-room hotel on the property next to the Sands

◆   Caribbean, a 388-room hotel/casino on Flamingo Road

◆   Circus-Circus plans construction of a 4,000-room hotel on the site of the present Hacienda, one of the oldest properties on The Strip

◆   Millenium, two or three megaresorts on 73 acres south of the Hacienda are also planned by Circus Circus. The result will be a solid stretch of Circus Circus properties from Excalibur at the corner of Tropicana and Las Vegas Boulevard S. to the corner of Las Vegas Boulevard and Russell Road.

◆   Chateau, a Mediterranean-themed hotel/casino with 400 rooms at Alta and Rampart in northwest Las Vegas

◆   Kactus Kate's, a 450-room hotel/casino on Rancho Blvd. near Fiesta, Texas and Santa Fe hotel/casinos

◆ Shan-Gri-La, a $40 million, futuristic casino combining several smaller downtown properties including Nevada and Queen of Hearts

◆ A million square-foot factory outlet mall

◆ The renovation and reincarnation of Sassy Sally's Casino (32 E. Fremont; 702-382-5777) into Rattlesnake Jack's

In telling you about future plans, we've dismissed those that are merely street talk at this time. But in Las Vegas, street talk is often on target, so there's probably even more to look forward to. And it's almost impossible to imagine what that might be.